Daffy definitions for seniors

WITH A LAUGH AND A PRAYER

BERNADETTE MCCARVER SNYDER

with illustrations from Chris Sharp

TWENTY THIRD *23rd*
PUBLICATIONS
NEW LONDON, CT 06320
WWW.23RDPUBLICATIONS.COM

TWENTY-THIRD PUBLICATIONS
A Division of Bayard
One Montauk Avenue, Suite 200
New London, CT 06320
(860) 437-3012 or (800) 321-0411
www.23rdpublications.com

ISBN 978-1-58595-846-7
Printed in the U.S.A.

Library of Congress Cataloging-in-Publication Data
Snyder, Bernadette McCarver.
Daffy definitions for seniors : with a laugh and a prayer.
p. cm.
ISBN 978-1-58595-846-7
1. Older people—Prayers and devotions. 2. Life—Humor. 3. Aging—Humor—
Dictionaries. 4. Old age—Humor—Dictionaries. 5. Older people—Humor—
Dictionaries. I. Title.
BV4580.S685 2011
242'.65—dc23
2011038260

DEDICATION

God speaks to each of us as he makes us,
Then walks with us silently out of the night.

These are the words we dimly hear:
You, sent out beyond your recall,
go to the limits of your longing.

Embody me.

Flare up like flame
and make big shadows I can move in.

Let everything happen to you: beauty and terror.
Just keep going. No feeling is final.
Don't let yourself lose me.

Nearby is the country they call life.
You will know it by its seriousness.

Give me your hand.

◆ RAINER MARIA RILKE'S BOOK OF HOURS, I, 59 ◆

I dedicate this book to all seniors who
see beauty and know terror, yet keep going.

And I pray, hold my hand.

Introduction

Down in the dumps? Despondent?

Well, at your ripe old age, maybe you have the right to feel that way. But maybe not!

According to statistics, there will soon be seventy-seven million senior citizens in America alone. And plenty of them are loving life and being grateful for every new day they are given.

If you are one of the grateful ones, hooray for you! And if you are one of the grouches, maybe you have good reason to frown and grumble. BUT, if you have been enjoying playing the victim and seeing only the downside of aging, then please STOP IT! In spite of the symptoms of senioritis, you probably just need a hot fudge sundae, a phone chat with a daffy, dauntless friend—or who knows, maybe you need this dictionary!

This book is not a prescription for sudden perfect health or a guaranteed trouble-free old age. It's just meant to give you a giggle so you can sometimes laugh at your knee that creaks or your brain that sometimes gets stuck in reverse. It might even be a step stool to help you climb up out of any doldrums or to change that burned-out light bulb in your age-challenged attitude.

I HOPE you'll enjoy the giggles and find enough impish inspiration in this book to share with others, and I hope you'll then agree that laughter really IS the best medicine.

aaah

Aaah is what the doctor tells you to say when he pushes a stick down your throat. You might feel like biting off that stick, but you're supposed to relax and keep saying aaah.

Senior life is supposed to give you better ways to relax and a bit more free time than you had when you were swashbuckling through the day, often demanding your rights and, if things didn't go your way, making like a Pirate and saying "Argh!" instead of "Aaah."

Now's the time to trade in your pirate eye-patch for a telescope so you can look around and clearly see all the possibilities to turn senior years into the new "wonder years." Take time to really relax, close your eyes and truthfully meditate on all the GOOD things in your life. Then gratefully have an aaah moment.

Dear Lord, sometimes now I think someone may be trying to stick something down my throat, expecting me to swallow it just because I'm old. Help me, Lord, to know when I should be suspicious and when I should NOT be. Give me wisdom, Lord, to know the difference between the time for an ARGH and for an Aaah.

AAAH!

alias

Do you know anyone who has an alias? Do you think people with an alias always have their picture on the post office wall? Well, how about you? If you have reached a certain age, you might have collected several aliases—student, doctor, teacher, repair person, parent, cook, dishwasher, retiree, or maybe grumpy complainer. Recognize any of those? Think today of what alias would be your favorite? How about Best Friend, Patient Listener, Fun Grandparent?

What about an alias you WISH you could claim? Maybe it's not too late to earn that one. Maybe it's time to think about how to work on adding a new one to your alias list—just be sure it's not an alias that would get your picture on the post office wall!

Dear Lord, today's world offers so many more opportunities for "mature" people than it did in the past. Added years do not signal time to just sit in a rocker and reminisce. Of course, that can be fun, too—but it IS limiting. Send the Holy Spirit to advise seniors to know whether it's time to volunteer, study, pray, or "adventure" more. Rockers are good—but rockets can light up a life with new ideas.

ambergris

Ambergris is a waxy substance that comes from whales, a gooey something that has a greasy-sounding name. But what do you guess this "gris" is used for? It cannot be used to fry hamburgers, to lubricate your car, or to oil a squeaky door. But it CAN be used to make perfume! Long ago, Arab fishermen noticed that ambergris had a sweet odor and they discovered it could be used in perfume as a "fixative" to make the aroma last longer. Some people love perfume and slosh it on so generously that even after they have left a room, you'll know they were there. They might be surprised to learn that their aroma lingers because it was made with waxy goo from a whale. Actually though, today neither whales nor nicely perfumed ladies have to worry about that much, because scientists have learned how to make synthetic ambergris.

Some seniors leave a lasting impression wherever they go—with or without perfume. They are always ready to volunteer their time to help family, friends, the parish, or the neighborhood. Those who have some physical problems and can't DO a lot for others, pray a lot for others—and sometime they just take the time to lend an ear to someone who needs to talk or they write an encouraging note. Help like that lingers long and can often make a whale of a difference in someone's life.

Dear Lord, when my son was about five years old, my mother came for a week's visit and the two of them had a fun time together. She was usually very frugal but not when it came to perfume. Her favorite one was a bit pricey, but she occasionally treated herself to it and I loved to get a whiff whenever she was near. One day I asked my son how he liked Grandma's perfume and he looked at me in surprise and said, "Grandma wears perfume? I just thought that was the way all old people smelled." Maybe that's the sweet smell of success.

bagatelle

A bagatelle is a trifle, a little doodad, a thing of little importance. Of course, some people might disagree with that definition. Some people might think a favorite small gift from a friend or a child's crayon drawing or the first star of night or the last jellybean in the jar are bagatelles. Others think they are treasures. Some people might think it is a little thing of no importance when they promise to do something for you or with you—and then don't bother to do it. YOU might think this is not a trifling matter. You might get your feelings hurt or decide never to trust that person again. Or maybe YOU might not keep a promise and somebody ELSE might get hurt. Think about the bagatelles in your life today. Which are trifling hurts that you hang on to but should let go? And which are true treasures like little kindnesses that can help wash away the hurts.

Dear Lord, people of all ages have lives filled with bagatelles. And sometimes they're so busy, it's hard for them to notice the difference between the trifles and the treasures. Help them, Lord. Help us all.

baggage

This term was once used to describe suitcases, trunks, and personal belongings of travelers. Those belongings included things such as a heavy coat, a purse, a briefcase, and maybe a book or magazine to read on the trip. But then one day people began to travel with laptops, skis, golf clubs, baby strollers, huge mystery packages tied up with strings, and evidently ALL of their favorite things.

This probably began when a very smart person figured out how to put wheels on suitcases. No longer were you limited to only two hands to carry everything. You could pile bag on bag on bag and pull it along after you. Actually that was a wonderful invention that made carting a suitcase so much easier. But people, as usual, carried it too far. Recently, security worries have slowed down but not stopped this urge to travel with everything you've ever owned.

In the same way, some people travel with a different kind of baggage, carrying around all their sins and worries and problems from the past, never leaving home without them. And some seniors are particularly dedicated to this type of travel. They've become old enough to know better and should have slain all those dragons of yesterday by now. But it's never too late. Senior years are a good time to atone or try to make peace with the past. It's not easy to put wheels on that kind of baggage but if done sincerely, it can make the senior journey much happier.

Dear Lord, please inspire seniors to not let the past ruin the present. Tell them to let go of all the old baggage so they can start to travel light and light-hearted.

basenji

A basenji is a "bark-less" dog that CAN make a howling sound but seldom does. There is also a New Guinea "singing" dog that sometimes makes a melodic yodeling sound. But MOST dogs are the barking kind. And most are a family's best friend. Those dogs offer unconditional love and free forgiveness. Even if you forget to feed your dog and his supper is late or you get too busy to talk to him when he wants to talk to you or you get mad and shout at him, as soon as you "are available" a dog is ready to be your best friend again. How many humans offer unconditional love and instant forgiveness? No wonder so many families and so many seniors have doggie best friends—whether they howl, sing, or just bark a lot.

Do you ever get up in the morning and feel like barking at everybody you meet? Nobody seems to know why some days start out right and you feel like singing and other mornings make you feel like growling or grumbling. The next time you have "one of those days," why don't you PRETEND you're a basenji—and keep your bark to yourself!

Dear Lord, I'm afraid I sometimes have "one of those days" and the only good thing about that is that after I do a bit of growling and grumbling, I realize I should take time out to talk to YOU. That means I have a longer than usual visit with you that day—and that helps take the bite out of my bark.

balloon

A balloon is an airtight bag filled with hot air. Does this mean a senior who is full of hot air is a balloon? No, but you might find such a person at events where there ARE balloons—retirement parties, garage sales, parades, or other kinds of celebrations or get-togethers. But just a minute. Did you know there are different meanings for this word? In chemistry, a balloon is a round vessel with a short neck. Hmm. That could also describe some seniors. But let's don't go there. In architecture, a balloon is a ball or a globe at the top of a pillar. In weaving, it's a reel on which yarn is wound. And in a cartoon, it's the outline that encloses the words said by a cartoon character. The next time you encounter a person full of hot air, imagine you see a balloon above his or her head and think of what words you would like to put there to describe the tirade. Or maybe the next time YOU are tempted to spout forth some hot air, think twice and stick a pin in your balloon before someone else does.

Dear Lord, spouting hot air is not reserved for seniors alone although we get a reputation for it. We've had more years to come up with pet peeves and favorite aggravations, so sometimes we just have to let it all out. Help us, Lord, to speak up when we have something that needs to be said but give some of those pet peeves a rest so we won't add to one of the many senior stereotypes.

balneology

Balneology is the science of bathing. I bet you didn't know taking a bath is a science! (Or maybe you discovered it IS a science if you have arthritis.) Actually, balneology means the kind of bathing that is therapeutic—the kind used to help heal or soothe. Suppose you strained a muscle (and you probably have). The doctor might tell you to spend some time in a nice warm bath to soothe the muscle and help it heal. Or suppose you had to have surgery on a knee or hip or funny bone. Afterward you might have to soak the "repaired" area in a whirlpool kind of bath.

Well, let's hope you never or at least seldom have to discover this science. But if you do find yourself in hot water, at least treat yourself to an interesting bathing suit—purple with yellow polka-dots for example. Then you can treat the other water-therapy folks to a good laugh—and they probably need one. OR you can "treat" them to a long treatise on the meaning of the word balneology!

Dear Lord, it doesn't take a scientist to tell anyone of a certain age about the scientific fact of how the human body can disappoint you by evolving into a whole new life form. Whether you want to or not, you find out how the hip bone may not be properly connected to the leg bone or how the head bone can suddenly freeze out and delete the memory of your best friend's phone number. But thank you, Lord, that today medical science DOES have so many new therapies and medicines and solutions to problems that help us elders ease on down the road. Thank you, thank you.

battery

What happens when the battery "goes dead" in your watch, your radio, your cell phone, or your flashlight? No time, no music, no conversation, no light! Those little batteries don't look like much but they can cause BIG irritation—especially if you forgot to buy some backups. So you can be thankful today for a man named Allessandro Volta, the physics professor who invented the first electric battery in 1800. Since then, scientists have developed batteries that come in all kinds of shapes and sizes—to give power to the things that you use in everyday life. And in case you ever wondered, electrical power is now measured in units called "volts" in honor of that inventive professor.

Do you ever have a day when you feel like your battery has gone dead—or is at least napping? That's when it's time to get yourself up, shake yourself about, and start all over again! I know it's a lot harder than it sounds, but you can't just sit there and mope, waiting for a lightning bolt to come through the window and hit your recharge button. Call a cheerful friend, go out to lunch, watch a happy movie, get a new hair cut, or just go to a store that sells greeting cards and read all the funny ones. Can't hurt. Might help.

Dear Lord, it's strange how a person's battery can suddenly die out for no reason. The bills are paid, nothing dire has happened, nobody has rained on your parade and yet, the old fizz has fizzled. Why did you make people with batteries that get tired for no reason? Are you just testing us, Lord, to see if we will realize that a napping battery is a sign we should check in with you—so you can give us a jump-start with your unending electricity of love.

"I THINK MY BATTERY JUST WENT DEAD"

caboodle

Caboodle means a group or a bunch of things—like all your STUFF! Evidently this word is a combination of kit, meaning family and friends, and boodle meaning your earthly possessions. Some seniors have a lot of both. Some don't. Some have things stuffed in the attic, the basement, the garage, and every drawer or closet in the house. Some don't. Some seem to spend more time or put more value on their kit. Some are too busy with their boodle. Which kind are you?

THINGS are great to have—a warm bed to sleep in, a dependable car, comfortable shoes to walk wherever or to prop up on a footstool. But there's a lot of STUFF you could live without. You probably could even live without family or friends but it's nice to have some—to laugh at your jokes, give you an occasional hug, listen to your worries, and offer help when you need it. If you spend too much time with your boodle, you won't have enough left to tell God thanks for all the blessings you already have. So use your noodle—put your kit before your boodle.

Dear Lord, I have noticed that some of the happiest people don't necessarily have the best or the most of everything. They just make the best or the most of whatever they have. Help me remember that, Lord, and help me find more time to spend with you and more energy to clean out the STUFF that is in my garage, closets, and drawers—and yes, in my head too!

caboose

This word is often used to describe anything or anyone who "brings up the rear." Of course it's also the name for that jazzy-looking little car that often is at the end of a train. It MIGHT be fun to ride in a caboose but it usually is NOT fun to be last—to be chosen last for a team, to come in last in a race, to be included as a last resort.

And it might not be pleasant to have people think you are on your last legs or keep reminding you that you are approaching or already IN the last phase of life. Well, just a doggone minute! It's quite an accomplishment to even REACH the last phase of life. Some people don't even make it that far. If you do, you have been given a gift of days—days to be spent complaining or days to spend gratefully accepting and even rejoicing. It's up to you. You can grouch about the gift not being good enough or you can enjoy "bringing up the rear." Didn't the Bible say something about "the last shall be first"? Hmmm… something to think about.

Dear Lord, help me remember that going first class is nice but even if you're in the caboose you're still traveling, so just sit back and enjoy the trip.

camel

A camel is an animal that is one of the world's most astonishing creatures. Someone once joked that a "camel is a horse put together by a committee" because it seems like a strange assortment of mismatched parts. Actually, the one-humped Arabian camel IS a masterpiece of nature. It can travel for miles without water and survive the savage sun and scorching winds of the desert. It has its own "sunglasses"—thick bushy eyebrows and long eyelashes—that protect its eyes from the blowing desert sand. For short distances, it can carry up to one thousand pounds—MORE than an elephant! And it will eat almost anything, including its owner's tent! Mark Twain once said, "I expect it would be a real treat to a camel to have a keg of nails for dinner."

Unfortunately, camels are also stubborn, sullen, bad-tempered, and easily offended. When they get mad at a camel driver, they often get even by biting, spitting, or trampling on his feet. So, like most people, the camel has its good traits and its bad ones. You probably don't know many

"No spitting!"

people who have the camel's good traits but you may know people who have some of the bad ones.

> *Dear Lord, you must have had fun making a camel, especially without a committee to help you. And maybe you put in some bad traits because you thought all that endurance in the desert earned the camel a way to get even. Thanks, Lord, for giving us an example of endurance AND the example of how NOT to get even like a camel.*

campanology

Campanology could have something to do with camping—but it doesn't. This word means the art of ringing bells. Bells have always been associated with churches because many churches had bell towers and a bell-ringer would pull on a long heavy rope to ring the huge bells in the tower. Sometimes these bells would be rung to announce it was time for prayer or for a wedding or a funeral. The bells could also be rung to alert people to some big disaster or emergency so they could come running to the church to find out what was happening. (This of course, was before the six o'clock news program or instant messaging began to spread the word in a different way.)

Today there are also bell-ringers INSIDE the church, ringing bells as the choir sings, which may be easier than hanging onto a heavy rope tied to a bell in the belfry. Or it might be harder since you have to ring in tune and on time! Some seniors have found bell-ringing to be a pleasant retirement activity. Some of those don't realize they are engaged in campanology. And if they ring the bell at the wrong time, they may wish they had engaged in camping instead of bell-ringing. Would YOU like to be a bell-ringer or would you prefer to wait till you hear the bell on an ice cream truck coming down your street so you can run out and engage in the art of ice-creaming?

Dear Lord, thank you for all those who have praised you in the past and now praise you in the present by bell-ringing, both in church and in the belfry.

cane

The word "cane" has many meanings. There's sugar cane that can some day sweeten your cup of tea. There's the kind of cane once used to punish misbehaving students—but thankfully is no longer in use. There's the cane that can be woven into baskets. And there's the cane otherwise known as a walking stick and sometimes considered by seniors to be a four-letter word. Yes, an unfriendly four-letter word. Even legs that could have once posed for pin-up pictures can betray you and stop supporting you at a certain age. That's when doctors or therapists might strongly urge you to carry a cane as a safety measure to possibly keep you from falling and breaking something. But everybody knows that if you use a cane, you might possibly be considered as aged and everybody knows that is another four-letter word that does not apply to you. It's OK for a younger person who is recovering from a sports injury to use a cane but certainly not for a spunky senior!

Of course, some seniors gladly accept a cane and sometimes find a fancy carved one or even decorate a regulation one with ribbons or what-nots and then step along like a fashion model. Others may use the cane at home but "forget" it and leave it in the car when they arrive at a social occasion. To cane or not to cane—that is definitely a serious senior conundrum.

> *Dear Lord, to each his own. Every senior has a personal lifestyle and a picture of herself or himself that cannot be trifled with. A cane may be a practical helpful addition to a wardrobe or it may be a threat to a psyche. Help seniors face reality, Lord, and decide honestly whether they cane or cane-not.*

centenarians

They belong to an exclusive Century Club. They are older than Mickey Mouse, the invention of television, or even crossword puzzles. And their numbers are growing. In 1990, according to the Census Bureau, there were 38,300, but by 2009, there were 104,099 seniors who had celebrated with 100 candles on a birthday cake. One of them said, "I have been blessed but I also had to work on it. You've got to work, have a cheerful attitude, and look for something fun to do."

One man lived independently until, at the insistence of his family, he moved into Assisted Living at age ninety-nine. One lady still does yoga, takes a half-hour walk before breakfast, enjoys a cocktail each evening before a home-cooked meal, and shares an apartment and KP duties with a younger friend who is only eighty-four. Another lady only recently gave up a lifelong passion for horseback riding but says, "I have no high blood pressure, diabetes, or high cholesterol but I am a bionic woman—with a pacemaker, hearing aids, and contact lenses."

Some had a hardscrabble existence in early years and all struggled through the Great Depression but they overcame obstacles and traumas by being resourceful and resilient. Many still have an acute memory and most have a healthy dose of self-esteem and strong ties to friends and family. As one lady said, "I just had a joyous life and a wonderful husband to have fun with and now I'm having a fun old age but I do seem to be getting a bit rustier by the day."

Dear Lord, the Century Club members have a lot to teach the sixty-seventy-year-old youngsters about how to remain joyous even as you get a bit rustier. Bless them all, Lord, and thanks for their examples.

CREAK!
CREAK!

clock

A clock is an instrument for measuring time and then showing you what time it is—so you'll know whether you're early or late or just in time for dinner. Long ago the only way people measured time was by sunrise and sunset. They got up when it got light and worked until it got dark. Then people began to invent interesting things—the sundial, the hourglass, the windup clock, the electric clock, AND the wrist watch—so you could have time on your hands. Now there's even an atomic clock that mysteriously resets itself some way when daylight saving time starts. Some seniors have too much time on their hands and others are so busy they never have enough. But it's important to think about how you MEASURE whatever amount of time you have each day. Do you measure it by how much work you get done? By how many prayers you said? By how many things you learned? By how much fun you had? Time is precious. Measure it well. Spend it wisely.

Dear Lord, some people don't even need a clock any more. They can find out what time it is by listening to the radio, watching TV, looking at the dashboard on the car, looking at a passing billboard, or just checking that good-looking watch on the wrist or that tiny little iPad, iPod, or iPhone in the pocket. Time marches on, no matter where we look for it.

derring-do

Derring-do is a way to describe someone who dares to do! However, this term is usually for one who chooses "to do" in a reckless or dashing fashion—like the movie pirate who brandishes a sword as he leaps from the deck of one ship to another or the policeman who leaps from rooftop to rooftop to catch a criminal or a detective who pursues a suspect in one of those crazy movie car chases. Derring-do can be exciting in a movie, but in real life it can be dangerous OR necessary. People who need chemotherapy treatments have to be brave to "do" this when it's necessary. Others have to bravely undergo treatment and therapy for broken bones, operations, and other frightening ailments. Some are faced with the loss of income, the loss of insurance for those costly medical bills, the loss of a longtime home, or the loss of friends who keep dying on them when they are not ready to let them go. Yes, derring-do has a whole new kind of definition in elderly years but it still requires daring to do!

> *Dear Lord, getting old can be even scarier than watching a derring-do movie, but with a little laugh and a big prayer, even serious problems can still be exciting if you face them as a chance to learn and to discover.*

dibble

Did you know a dibble is a pointed tool which you use to dig holes in the ground so you can plant seeds, young plants, or bulbs? No, not light bulbs—no matter how carefully you plant them, they never grow into a candelabra. But if you plant tulip bulbs, they might grow into a beautiful bouquet that would look lovely in the light of your candelabra or even by the light of that candle that you have tried to burn at both ends. Of course, you don't have to have a dibble to plant something in the garden. You can use a shovel or even an old tablespoon. But maybe a dibble might just be the pointed tool to convince you to shake the doldrums and plant something NEW in your life. Is it time to try a hobby you may have always wished to have time to try? Could you plan a short weekend trip to a place you always wanted to visit? Would you like to sign up for a class at a senior center or join a Bible study group or take piano lessons? Who knows what kind of dibbles and bits you might find when you dig deep down into that idea box of possibilities?

Dear Lord, senior years can be the best time for harvesting new ways to liven up your life. But—like all good things—they don't usually just pop up. You have to use a dibble and then follow your own candelabra.

dig

To dig means to break up, loosen, or turn earth with some kind of implement. Of course, it can also mean to dig up some dirt about someone, to dig down and delve into a mystery to bring some clue or fact to light, or to really "dig" someone or some thing you like or admire. On my desk, it usually means to dig through a pile of papers, clippings, bills, or recipes to find something needed IMMEDIATELY!

At a certain age, it's important to keep on digging—to drag out old photographs and give them to some younger relatives so they can see how cute we all looked (or thought we did at the time!), to dig through closets and donate usable things so someone else can enjoy them, to dig into your old address book and call or write an old friend just to have fun recalling some silly times you shared. All of those are more productive than digging in your heels over an old hurt or thinking up a way to get in some not-nice digs about a neighbor or relative. So get out your shovel and dig into today with a smile on your face and a positive attitude and have a hot-diggity-dog good time.

Dear Lord, I love looking through my old photo albums and remembering all the crazy fun times we had but it's even more fun to look through my mother's album full of black and white photos and see how the folks dressed waaay back when. But as for that pile on my desk, Lord, it's beginning to look like an archaeological dig so help me get out my shovel today and dig in.

dynamite

Dynamite was a bang-up idea invented by Alfred Nobel in 1867. He probably thought it would be a very helpful thing for the world because you could use it to clear the way to build new roads or buildings. For example, you could blast out a huge rock in a construction site very quickly. But some people used his discovery to DESTROY things and sometimes hurt people. Nobel probably felt bad about this and that may be the reason he established the famous NOBEL PRIZE. This prestigious award is given each year to people who have done something "distinguished" in the fields of chemistry, economics, physics, medicine, literature, or physiology. AND a special Nobel Prize is given to the person who has done the most each year to promote world peace. Today many seniors are honored for doing something "distinguished" in many different fields and many are known for being the peacemaker in their family, if not in the world. Nobel would probably be happy to know that it is now a compliment when people like that are described as being DYNAMITE!

Dear Lord, blowing up things can be an important part of any kind of construction project today, but blowing up and saying something hurtful is still possible in every age group. As the saying goes, Lord, please give us patience—but hurry!

earmark

Earmark does not mean something ridiculous—like sticking a banana in your ear! Instead, it's a mark of identification or distinction. It was first used when the EARS of cattle were MARKED with their owner's special brand so if the animals got out and roamed the range, the cattlemen could identify which ones were whose property. Today this term is used to signify something that is to be set apart—like earmarking a certain amount of money to take a trip to Hawaii or a trip to the dentist. And then the word earmark is now used in politics, but let's not go there.

Some people also seem to have a special earmark that sets them apart. They have a special way of talking, walking, laughing, raising their eyebrows or furrowing their brow. Do you think you have an earmark? Maybe you have a special way of noticing, listening, helping, or cheering up others! A lot of people of maturity have those kinds of earmarks—and hooray for them.

Dear Lord, some days I think I SHOULD put a banana in my ear just to get the attention of those you-know-whos who are NOT good at noticing, listening, helping, or cheering. Forgive me, Lord. I know that sometimes I am one of those you-know-whos. Help us all.

eccentric

Eccentric describes something that is irregular, off the center, out of the ordinary. Do you know anyone or anything that is eccentric? Some people thought Jesus was eccentric. He didn't do things in the ordinary way. He told people to "love your enemies." What? Instead of hating them? He said that if someone hurts you, you should "turn the other cheek." What? Instead of hitting back or getting even? He said to "love your neighbor as yourself." What? Even that grouchy one who looks the other way when you wave and smile? Some of the things Jesus taught certainly were and ARE eccentric, irregular—and wonderful.

But now wait a minute! Think about that last one. How can you love your neighbor when you don't love yourself? Maybe you have been feeling low because you can't do things you used to do the same way you used to do them. Then try doing them in a new easier way. You can't walk as fast or climb steps as fast as you did before? Well maybe it's time to just "take your time." You don't have to be as fast as before. You don't have to be perfect. You should appreciate who you are and what you are. You ARE special. You ARE loved by God. And you should be thankful for your good qualities while trying to improve the not-so-good ones. THEN, when you accept the new/old you, it will be easier to appreciate and love your family, friends, AND your neighbors too—the way eccentric Jesus told everyone to do.

Dear Lord, some of my favorite friends are eccentric— and they probably think I am too. We accept each other and have a lot of fun being old and still doing things in an irregular, off the center way. Sometimes others shake their heads and laugh at us—and that's just fine—it's great to still be able to give someone a good laugh!

electricity

Electricity is something that we probably could not live without in this new technologically-oriented society. No electric light, no TV, no computer, no electric eye to open doors for us, no electric checkout machines to tell us how much lunch cost! Oh no! We have become totally dependent on this amazing invention that rules our current world. Did you know that Benjamin Harrison was the first president to put electricity in the White House—but he and his wife were both afraid to touch the switches! Well, it must have seemed frightening when electricity first began to do "magic" things. And it's even more frightening now when we think what the world could be without it. Sure, our ancestors did OK with candles to light, ink pens to write, wood fires to cook or heat. But we are too spoiled to go back to that. Every time a storm knocks down some electric wires and we are left in the dark, we have little patience with the electric company, wanting our lights back on NOW. The good old days may seem perfect when we recall them, but if we had to go back to living without our cell phones, garage door openers, electric coffee pots, and microwave ovens, we would truly think we were living in the Dark Ages.

Dear Lord, forgive us for becoming so dependent, so soft, so unlike our forefathers and foremothers. We like to brag about our liberty, our independence, but when the lights go out, we wimpy ones lose our electric personalities. Thank goodness we can always depend on you, Lord, without needing an extension cord to get in touch.

elephant

Whether you've seen an elephant up-close or in a movie or on TV, you know how to define or describe one—it's a BIG animal with a proboscis that is called a trunk for some unknown reason. You may have also noticed that an elephant has four strong legs as big as tree stumps attached to huge feet. But did you know that elephants can't jump? Elephants have the same kind of bones in their feet as other animals do, but elephant foot bones are packed closer together so they DON'T have the same kind of "spring" mechanism that helps other animals jump. It's probably a good thing. Can you imagine what it would be like if you were at a circus and a lot of elephants started jumping up and down? It would feel like an earthquake. And besides, God probably made the elephants that way because they don't play basketball and they evidently never have the need to jump!

Now you, on the other hand, have had the need to hop, skip, and jump in your lifetime. You have needed to jump when a good opportunity presents itself, to jump up and down in an exercise class or jump over tall building blocks in a single bound when you came across kids' toys left in the middle of the floor. After years of all that jumping, maybe your spring mechanism may be getting a bit rusty. But don't let that get you down. If you have a positive attitude, you can still always be ready to jump for joy!

Dear Lord, recently I've been doing most of my jumping from a comfy chair—when it's my turn to "jump" while playing a board game or when I'm reading the paper and hear a loud noise in the kitchen which means something in my overstocked, unorganized pantry has fallen to the floor. Sounds like it's time for me to pack my trunk, get back into the exercise jungle, and do some jumping jacks.

Elephant Ears

A nice green plant which you might see inside the house or outside, has taken on the name of Elephant Ears because its green leaves are as big as an elephant's ears. This plant must have gotten its name from tropical Africa because the elephants there are the ones with those big floppy ears. The elephants who live in the forests of southeastern Asia have relatively small ears. Did you know that? Do you know anyone who has large "better to hear you with, my dear" ears? Well, don't mention it. They already became aware of that when the kids in grammar school pointed it out.

Kids have a way of labeling someone with a nickname that has nothing to do with the real person. Sometimes elders do the same, making fun of the way the grandkids talk or walk or think. And these "fun" nicknames sometimes stick. And sometimes they hurt, they are embarrassing, they leave someone labeled improperly. Of course, some nicknames are cute and/or charming and were never meant to be hurtful. But this is a good example of how making fun is not always funny.

Dear Lord, I have a photo of my grandfather (who died before I was born) and he had real stick-out-from-the-head ears. The "studio-type" posed photo shows him sitting straight as an arrow in suit and tie with a small flower in his buttonhole, looking as distinguished as his honorary title—Squire McCarver. Somehow, I doubt anybody ever tried calling him "Elephant Ears" and I hope they didn't.

elevator

An elevator is a contraption that can lift people or things either up or down. The first elevator for people was invented by Elisha Graves Otis in 1857. Fifteen years later, William LeBaron Jenney designed the first skyscraper—a ten-story building. Can you guess why no one had ever built a skyscraper before?

Well, why would anyone build a ten-story building when no one had invented an elevator yet? Sometimes one good invention triggers another. Today there are much taller buildings all over the world—and they all have elevators.

Some days when you are feeling very loooow, don't you wish somebody would invent an elevator that could lift your spirits and make you feel like singing or dancing or flying to the moon? There's only one person who could invent such an elevator—and that person is YOU. When you get down, go ahead and let yourself feel really baaad for a while—maybe even cry a few tears or stomp your feet, feeling sorry for yourself. Then when you're all finished with that, wash your face and hit the UP button. Say a little prayer, eat a little ice cream, watch a funny program on TV, and lift your own spirits. Think about all the HAPPY things in your life and then raise up your head and shout, "GOING UP!" and then GO!

"Now
THAT'S
UPLIFTING"

Dear Lord, I know all that is easier said than done but if you let yourself sink deeper into a funk, that's not as much fun as pretending you are an elevator!

English

English is a language spoken by more than 350 million people. It is an important—and confusing—language. Suppose you were trying to teach another person to speak English and you told him about the words hear (something you do with your ears) and here (where you are right now) but explained that both words SOUND alike but are spelled differently and have different meanings. That would be confusing! And THEN you'd have to tell them about seen and scene, red and read, peer and pier, dear and deer. Oh dear! See how confusing English could be if you didn't already know it? Sometimes it's confusing even if you DO know how to speak it—you say something nice but someone misunderstands and thinks you MEANT something not nice. It's even worse if you DID mean to say something not nice.

But you're old enough to know not to do that, aren't you? Well, remember the old saying, "Be careful what you dish out today because tomorrow you might have to eat your words."

Dear Lord, no matter how old one gets, it is still so easy to speak now, think later. I'm so glad that I don't have to be so careful when I speak to you, Lord, because you can sort through the words I use and know what I am really trying to say. Thanks for that.

exercise

Exercise has several definitions. One is "bodily exertion for the sake of developing physical fitness." In other words, exercise is something you do to try to add some hop, skip, and jump into your life instead of flop, drop, and slump. There are only two things you HAVE to do to live an ordinary life: eat and sleep. BUT if you don't want to be physically phfffft, you have to do SOME exercise. Health experts say if you get enough exercise, you won't have so many aches and pains and won't be so likely to feel sluggish, dejected, or bored. If the only exercise you get is pushing the buttons on the TV remote, step outside and exercise your lungs by drinking in some of that fresh only-slightly-polluted air, exercise your legs by walking to the mailbox, exercise your eyes by looking to see what your neighbor is up to, and exercise your mind by thinking of all the good things in your life that don't require exercise. There! Don't you feel better already?

Dear Lord, I'm kidding about exercise but I know it is really important—especially for aging bodies. But I also know that the most important kind is a routine of meditating or saying certain prayers every day—a SPIRITUAL exercise for aging minds and souls. That really CAN make you "feel better already!"

"WHAT'S ALL THAT CREAKING?"

frog

A frog is a grown-up tadpole! There are bullfrogs, leopard frogs, and even tree frogs. Frogs leap and sleep and can often be found near water   or in somebody's throat. Did you ever get a sore throat and your voice sounded all husky and funny and you explained it by saying, "I've got a frog in my throat." Now why would you say that? Because everybody else says that. But why? It seems that way back in the Middle Ages when no one knew much about medicine, doctors had some strange practices. If someone got a throat infection, doctors would sometimes put a live frog, head first, into a patient's mouth. They thought the frog would inhale and breathe the infection into itself and out of the patient! It was not a pleasant experience for the patient OR the frog but ever since, people have been using the expression "frog in my throat" to describe a throat problem. Isn't it surprising how people accept old "sayings" and love old antiques and still like old songs but they are sometimes uncomfortable about being around old people? Maybe they think aging is catching—and maybe it is. If you "think" old, you'll start acting old and before you know it, you might have an old frog in your throat!

> *Dear Lord, it's wonderful that doctors and scientists have made great leaps in medical discoveries and new treatments. That's the good news. The bad news is finding a way to swallow all the new medical costs! Oh well, it's hard to cough up enough money to pay the bills but that's a lot better than coughing up a you-know-what.*

grit

Grit can mean sand or gravel. Grits can be something you get for breakfast in a Southern restaurant (whether you want it or not.) Gritting your teeth (grinding them together) is what some people do when they are angry or worried or nervous or scared. Gritting your teeth is also what some people do when they are determined to do something or have an opinion and refuse to budge (this could be called having "true grit" or just being stubborn.) Then there's the word GRITH which means peace, security, safety, refuge—just the opposite of teeth gritting. Actually, in medieval England grith meant sanctuary—whether it was imposed or guaranteed under certain conditions. Bet you didn't know that because medieval England was before your time (no matter what the kids think!)

Well, it takes a lot of grit and some gritting of the teeth to handle all the "surprises" that pop up in senior years. But that's OK. Today's seniors are made of sturdy stuff and they know that sometimes it takes grit and gritting—and sometimes even a bowl of grits—to achieve "TRUE GRITH!"

Dear Lord, this is probably the first time in history that so MANY seniors have had the grit to live and function and enjoy life into the nineties and even beyond. Thank you, Lord, for helping them set a good example—whether the young people have the grit to follow it or not.

grudge

Grudge is an ugly-sounding word that means a feeling of deep-seated resentment or ill will that you carry around with you either secretly or while grumbling and complaining. It can also apply to something that you give up or give to someone reluctantly and grudgingly. You might be peeved at someone who got something you thought should be yours or who did or said something that offended you (maybe a looong time ago) but instead of forgiving or forgetting, you hung onto your anger and kept carrying around a grudge against the "offending" person.

Grudges usually make the grudger feel miserable so it hurts them more than the one they are grudging. If YOU have been holding a grudge or carrying one around with you, get rid of it! Yuck! Take a good look at it and see how ugly it is. Then throw that grudge away as far as you can. Who would want to hold on to something so ugly.

Dear Lord, help those who need to get rid of a long-time grudge. It may be very hard to do but it's worth doing. Sometimes to get rid of an ugly cancer or infection, you have to take treatments that are painful or swallow medicine that tastes awful and has bad side effects but you gotta do it to get well. And the same is true with a grudge. You gotta get rid of it, even if you do it grudgingly.

"THAT'S QUITE SOME GRUDGE YOU'RE CARRYING"

gum

Gum is something you chew. It exercises your jaws—and of course, everyone knows that exercise is GOOD for you! Some gums are flavored and taste good and make your breath smell better. And some gums are even bubble-makers! But did you know that you might not have chewing gum today if not for a notorious military general named Santa Ana?

Many years ago Texas belonged to Mexico but wanted to break away. There was a terrible battle and General Santa Ana lost and Mexico was forced to release Texas. After that, Santa Ana had to get out of Mexico so he moved to New York—and brought along his favorite "chew." It was called chicle and was the dried milky sap of the Mexican jungle tree known as the sapodilla. A New York inventor tried the General's chicle and decided he might invent a way to make money with it. He imported a big batch of chicle from Mexico and made it into little balls and put jars of them in drugstores and they were sold for a penny apiece. This new "chew" was a success and later flavoring was added to make cherry, peppermint, and even sassafras gum.

Today there are many different brands and flavors of gum and people like to chew gum when they ride a bike or watch a movie or work on a computer writing a book. Do you ever exercise your jaws by chewing gum? If you don't, you should because then you could tell people you are trying a wonderful new "exercise program" for seniors.

Dear Lord, who could imagine that a Mexican jungle tree and a notorious General could be the source for bubble gum? Ain't life grand!

hobby

A hobby is a favorite way to pass time. Maybe that's why they sometimes call it a pastime! It's also an enjoyable way to use spare time or something to do when there's nothing to do. The most popular hobby in the world is stamp collecting. But people also like to collect interesting or unusual types of things—shells, rocks, earrings, salt and pepper shakers, pens and pencils, funny hats, etc. And SOME people just collect dust balls under the furniture. Other hobbies include games like golf, bowling, checkers, or chess. Did you know there are 170,000,000,000,000,000,000,000,000 ways to play the ten opening moves in a game of chess? That's what the experts say—so somebody must have spent a long time counting them all. Maybe counting was his or her hobby.

Do YOU have a hobby? Maybe you're too busy already to find time for one but if you are not, maybe you should consider it. Folks of all ages enjoy simple hobbies like crossword puzzles, reading mysteries, knitting, or maybe collecting hobby horses!

"QUITE THE COLLECTION!"

There are probably 170,000,000,000,000,000,000,000,000,000 different hobbies you could choose. Isn't it exciting that life is so full of possibilities?

Dear Lord, some people have busy lives and obligations even after they are eligible for a senior discount. But for some who have a bit of spare time, a hobby can be an amusing and pleasant way to spend it. And even though it isn't a hobby, they can also spend time visiting with you and telling you about the 170,000,000,000,000,000, 000,000,00 problems OR joys in the days of their lives.

hogwash

Hogwash is NOT something you do to your pig on Saturday night! It's a senior kind of word that you might use to describe empty talk, foolish ideas, or anything YOU don't agree with. When anyone (like a young whipper-snapper) expresses an opinion that is NOT the same as yours, you might say HOGWASH to let that person know you think he or she is just not as brilliant as you are. OR you could just try to listen to the other person's opinion without any pre-prejudice affecting your reply. And who knows! You just might learn something.

Some of those new and crazy ideas have turned out pretty good in the past—like the telephone, the airplane, and even the computer. Although it might be depressing to try to deal with all the new ideas floating around today, try to become a good listener—instead of always hogging the conversation!

Dear Lord, thanks for silly words like Hogwash. They don't make much sense but it's kinda fun to say them. On those days, Lord, when things don't make much sense, remind us to stop and catch a breath and think of something that's kinda fun to think about—maybe words like higgledy-piggledy, bamboozle, flim-flam, alley-oop. Using a new word every day in conversation just might get the attention of those whipper-snappers.

hot dog

Hot-dogging can mean being a show-off or doing fancy stunts when you are maybe surfing or skiing. Now only a few people do that but lots of people enjoy that tasty meat-on-a-bun that is especially popular at a ballgame or cookout. But do you know why that treat is called a HOT DOG? There's a story—that may or may not be true—that many years ago there was a man who sold a new kind of sandwich at a ballpark. He called it "tube steak with mustard." Who would want to eat something called tube steak? It sounds like it was made out of an old tire. (Some hot dogs taste like that today—but that's another story.) In spite of its name, people tried it and LIKED it. The story goes that the tube-steak man was always accompanied by his old collie dog and on hot summer afternoons at the ballpark, the dog would start to pant and wilt under his collie hair and look very hot. Everybody noticed the old dog and started calling his owner "the hot dog man." Eventually, they started calling the hot dog man's sandwiches hot dogs. So that was a long story to get to an end. Some seniors (and some writers) can take a long time to spiel out a story. And some seniors still do some hot-dogging in spite of their age. So the next time you are served a hot dog, you might like to hot-dog by telling this story OR you might like to just smear on the mustard and enjoy your tube steak.

Dear Lord, you must get tired of all my long stories but your Bible has some long stories in it too and I enjoy them. So thanks, Lord, for long stories and hot dogs—and for collie dogs and mustard too.

hut

A hut is a very small cabin or house, sometimes far away in the woods. Some people live in huts because they don't have enough money to live in a regular house. Some people live in a hut only on weekends or vacations just to do something different, to "get away from it all—whatever "it" is. The famous writer George Bernard Shaw had a special "writing" hut where he would go to be alone to "write." HIS hut was built so it could spin on a pole to follow the sun! Wouldn't that be fun—to have a spinning hut? Well, wherever you live—in a house, hut, apartment, or palace—enjoy it and appreciate it. Many homeless people would be happy to have ANY kind of shelter to get in from the cold and rain. The next time you start to complain or feel bad because your home isn't big enough or fancy enough or warm enough or cool enough, stop and say a prayer of thanksgiving that you have SOME kind of hut to call home.

Dear Lord, today there are people of all ages who have lost their homes, their savings, their jobs—through no fault of their own. They have been good workers, frugal savers, careful care-takers of their home but once their jobs got down-sized, their savings got used up and their homes were foreclosed on. Please help them, Lord, to find jobs so they can once again be able to pay for a place they can call home.

hymn

A hymn can be a solemn song, a festive song, a song praising or glorifying God, a song that inspires or cheers. A hymn is usually sung in church but it CAN be sung anywhere YOU are there to sing it. Actually, hymn is a funny name for a song, isn't it? It sounds like it can only be sung by hims, not hers. But it's called that because it came from the Latin word hymnus that means song. We have a lot of English words that came from Latin words. If you had been naming a song to praise God, what would YOU have called it?

Would you have called it Hooray! Wow! Loveya! Fantastic! Thanksalot! Why don't you think about your favorite hymn today and see if you remember special lines that inspired you or uplifted you. If you don't know any hymns, make up one. And sing it out loud. This is a good day for singing because every day is a good day for singing.

Dear Lord, I love to sing out loud in church but that may not be inspiring or uplifting to those around me. I hope it's OK with you, Lord, because I heard that "to sing is to pray twice" and that's the way I feel about it. I love the words of some of the songs. Of course some of the hymns are better than others and I have to admit that only in my elder years did I really start to pay attention to the words instead of singing by rote. I realize now that many of them have such beautiful messages and they DO inspire and cheer me. Whether they are sung by hims or hers or both!

imagination

"I THINK HE'S GONE TO Fiji"

Imagination is a magic trick that lets you see something that isn't there, go somewhere you've never been, walk through a flower garden in the middle of a snowstorm, or go sledding on the hottest day of the summer. Imagination is a special gift that humans have and animals don't. Imagination can save you from boredom, free you from ordinariness, change a drab day into a fun time—and it may be the only way you can travel when you get older and can't walk or sled or dance the polka as well as you once did. So lucky you if you have a really great imagination. Use it, exercise it so it can grow stronger even if YOU don't! Use it to help you find a new way to solve an old problem in your life or make a plan to do something new in your life today or maybe some day in the near or distant future. And if you get stuck, ask an imaginative friend to help you look for a new goal, a project, a possibility. Dreams start with ideas and you know what they say—"you gotta have a dream or you'll never have a dream come true."

Dear Lord, with all the security measures and long lines at the airport today, traveling can be more difficult than in the past but if we use our imagination, we can always take a flight of fancy. Thanks for this special gift, Lord.

inch

An inch is a small amount, a measure of how tall you are or how round you are, a part of a dimension of a rug, a room, a sky-scraper. You can walk slowly enough to inch along or you can be daring and pull a stunt that brings you within an inch of your life.

What a big definition for such a small word. This reminds us of how important every thing on earth is, no matter how small. Just an inch can decide whether the sofa will fit. Just an inch too tall might determine whether you could become an astronaut. Just an inch too small might determine whether you could fit into last year's slacks. And that might remind you how important little things are, like the way you treat people—not just important people like your best friends but the grocery bagger, the trash man, even the IRS agent. The famous writer Maya Angelou once said, "I've learned that people will forget what you said, people will forget what you did, but people will never forget how you made them feel."

Dear Lord, help us be more careful about the way we

treat everyone we meet each day. It's an important
lesson to learn, even if it takes us an inch at a time.

insurance

This is something you pay a lot of money for but hope you never get to use. In today's uncertain world, you can buy insurance to protect you from fire, theft, auto accidents, tornadoes, floods, health problems affecting you and family, health problems of your dog or cat, an ugly lawn, broken teeth, broken fences, and maybe even broken promises. Yet with all this insurance of safety, nobody feels safe! Well, I guess it's a human thing. And maybe some seniors are guiltier than others. We're always waiting for the next shoe to fall, the next problem lurking around the corner to pounce. And what does all this worry achieve? Nada, nothing, no way, José. Of course, it's prudent in today's "you'll sue me if I don't sue you first" society to try to protect yourself—but not to extremes. In addition to our basic insurance, we should think of God as our most important insurance policy. Only God knows what's going to happen next week or maybe in the next minute and he doesn't even have insurance! He would have good reason to expect us all to be good loving children all our lives in gratitude for the many blessings he has given us—but are we? He has no insurance or assurance that we won't lie, cheat, steal, hurt others, or mess up his lovely world in some horrible way. How did God ever have the courage to create a whole world without taking out an insurance policy first?

Dear Lord, I'm talking silly again but you know what

I mean. We should be prudent to take care of ourselves and your planet but we should have faith in you as you have had faith in us. Thank you, Lord.

inventor

There are many famous inventors and one of the most famous of course is Thomas Edison. He invented the phonograph, the first commercially viable electric light, an experimental talking motion picture, and in New York City he built the world's first permanent electric power plant for distributing electric light. You probably knew all that but did you know that he patented more than 1,300 inventions? And did you know that many of his inventions were successful and made him famous but many MORE did NOT work—so he knew failure as well as success. If he had become discouraged by failure and quit experimenting, we would not be enjoying some of his successful inventions today. Most lives have some failures and some successes but you're never too old to rejoice in your successes and LEARN from your failures.

Dear Lord, so many things we use today are inventions that are spin-offs of Edison's first ones, so we should be grateful for him and for those inventors who followed him. Now if you could just put a little electric light in my head to wake me up today, Lord, I might be able to invent a way to clean the basement, do the laundry, find something in the back of the refrigerator that could turn into a delicious dinner, and get some checks in the mail. Light me up, Lord, light me up.

irritable

You want a definition for this word? Well, I could show you a picture of it if I took a photo of my face early some morning before the coffee has perked. Of course trying to do that would make me even more irritable because I'd have to find where I left the camera, turn on the lights, and try to remember how you work this silly new digital thing. It's not a bad idea though because when I looked at my own photo it would probably look so scary it would make me start laughing and soon I wouldn't be so irritable anymore. Do you ever laugh at yourself? It's good medicine and fun too.

Unfortunately some seniors tend to be a bit irritable—and that's why this word should remind us to be careful to "bite your tongue" when dishing out advice or criticism. Years of age do not always turn into years of wisdom. But sometimes they do. And it's important to share that wisdom with the next generation. But we are old enough to know the difference between lemon and lemonade so it's best to dish out our thoughts with a spoonful of sugar. And again, when you get exasperated too quickly, look in the mirror and try laughing at yourself.

Dear Lord, it's hard to not be critical of today's immodest fashions, immoral TV shows, and the immoderate spending habits of today's youth. But maybe it's hard for the younger folk to not be critical of some of the not-so-perfect behavior of seniors. Help us both, Lord. Help us know when it's time to bite the tongue or time to sugarcoat some wise advice.

jigsaw

Jigsaw is a special saw that can jiggle around and cut wood in
curvy or irregular lines. And a jigsaw puzzle is a picture that
has been cut into curvy or irregular lines so you can
have the fun of putting it back together again.
Do you know who made the first jigsaw
puzzle? More than 200 years ago, a
man named John Spilsbury thought
it would be fun to teach geography by playing a game. He
took slabs of wood and painted maps on them; then he cut
the maps along the boundary
lines of the countries or states.
Instead of just HEARING about
geography, his class had the fun of trying to figure out where
each country or state fit into the puzzle.

Since then there have been all kinds of jigsaw puzzles—
some with just a few pieces for small children and some with
5000 pieces for people who really like to get it all together!

Have you noticed how life is like a jigsaw puzzle? There are
lots of pieces and you have the work OR the fun of putting
them all together to make a pretty picture. As you get older, the
pretty picture you have put together should stay the same but it
doesn't always work that way. Somebody or some thing comes
along and jiggles the pieces and here you are trying to get it all
together again.

In a puzzle you have to put all the jiggled pieces back exactly
as they were before, but life is not that boring. If you work on

it and pray on it, sometimes when you put the new pieces into the picture it is even better than before.

Dear Lord, as the years pass by, the family picture is always changing—new in-laws enter, new babies are born, someone has an accident or illness that changes life drastically, someone has to move out of the family home into assisted living or a nursing home and the picture is not the same. Sometimes we get mad at you, Lord, wondering why you keep changing things. But we have to admit that it isn't your fault. It's just life. Even the atoms in our bodies and our planet are always changing and that's a sign of life. So forgive us, Lord, for wanting sameness. Help us welcome newness, new life, new answers to old puzzles.

jitterbug

This can often be sighted at Senior dances where couples may be observed jumping around like nervous or jittery bugs! Although this dance has a silly name and might look silly to watch, it's "a jazz derivation of the two-step in which couples swing, balance, and twirl in standardized patterns and often with vigorous acrobatics." Today some seniors might not be quite as acrobatic as in the past but they can still jitter with the music and it's a lot more fun than joining an exercise class. But there are some other bugs that are not as much fun like the bugs that get into your computer or the litterbugs that mess up the neighborhood and the planet, and the bugs that make people sick. And then there's a bug called a praying mantis and a praying bug MUST be a nice bug. And there's a lady bug so it must have nice manners. So watch your manners and say your prayers and whatever problem comes into your life today, don't let it bug you!

Dear Lord, it does seem that today's society has found so many new ways to make us jittery and so many technological wonders that really bug oldsters. Help us Lord to not let the small irritations keep us from enjoying the big picture. Teach us to just listen to the music of your blessings.

joke

A joke is something said or done to provoke laughter. Jokes draw our attention to the humorous or ridiculous things in life—and they often cheer up our mood or our day. As you probably know, there are lots and lots of senior citizen jokes now—some are not so nice, some cut too close to the bone, and some are really funny. You've probably heard them all but there's one that COULD actually happen so I'll pass it along.

A woman called and demanded to speak to her doctor. Surprisingly, he picked up the phone and she said, "Doctor, I just got the medicine you prescribed and the directions indicate that I will have to take this for the rest of my life. Is that correct?" In a soothing voice, the doctor replied, "Yes, I'm afraid that's true." In a distraught voice, the woman said, "Well, what ELSE are you not telling me, Doctor? This prescription says NO REFILLS!"

Hooray for the woman who demanded an answer from her doctor instead of just dissolving in a torrent of tears. Too often, communication between doctor and patient leaves a bit to be desired. Sometimes you can only leave a message for a doctor and only get an answer back from a nurse. Even when you are face to face at an appointment, you forget to ask important questions—and that's your fault. You need to be prepared with questions and the doctor should be prepared with answers.

So sometimes a joke points out a problem but at least it gives you a laugh at the end.

Dear Lord, some seniors are offended at all the jokes about aging but I love to hear them. It's very therapeutic to stop and laugh at yourself.

jumbo

Did you ever go to a circus? Did you like the clowns or the elephants? Did you know there was once a famous elephant named Jumbo? Way back in 1869, a hunting party captured one of the largest elephants ever seen in West Africa. He weighed six-and-a-half-tons and the natives called him by the Swahili word Jumbo, which meant chief. Jumbo became a favorite at the London zoo where thousands of school children took rides on his back. Then P. T. Barnum "discovered" Jumbo and bought him to perform in the "Barnum and Bailey Greatest Show on Earth." Jumbo became a huge hit in America and Barnum made Jumbo's name a synonym for anything "huge" in America and around the world.

Not too many years ago, when you went to the circus or a movie, you maybe got a small bag of popcorn and a small drink. Today wherever you go, you get a Jumbo everything. Barnum would be amazed! It's nice to live in a land of plenty but sometimes too much of a good thing is too much.

Dear Lord, thank you for so many riches in our lives and for circuses and entertainers and awesome animals like Jumbo, but remind us that moderation is best in most things and many good things come in small packages.

ketchup

Gimme a burger with onions, pickles, and lots of fish sauce. What? Yep, that's how ketchup first got its name—from a Chinese word that meant "pickled fish-brine or sauce." When Dutch traders first imported this "condiment" from the Orient, the English tried to make their own version by adding such things as cucumbers, mushrooms, walnuts, and yes, oysters. But it was the American seamen who took the then-popular sauce and added tomatoes from Mexico to turn it into TOMATO ketchup.

Through the years, it has been called ketchup, catsup, catch-up, and kitchup, but however you call it, it's become an American staple and every year, over half a billion bottles of it are slopped on everything from scrambled eggs to graham crackers. And you thought you had a complicated family history! Do YOU have a strange and interesting family story to tell? Then tell it before it disappears like pickled fish-brine. Kids may not want to hear your stories now but one day they'll wish they had listened more closely. One of your younger relatives might make a school project by hooking you up for an interview and tape or video you telling the wild and crazy or sweet and touching stories of your ancestors. In generations to come, the family could listen to or watch a TRUE story—in which YOU play a starring role!

Dear Lord, my family history includes stories of speakeasies in New York during Prohibition, ties with Franklin Roosevelt and Jimmy Carter, heroes and villains, and a dream my father had that changed us forever. The generation just behind me keep asking me to write it down but I've been too busy writing other things. Help me find time, Lord, to put my own ketchup story into the computer. And thanks, Lord, for all the days and all the stories you have given me.

kinderhook

Do you know what U.S. President Martin Van Buren has to do with Henry Hudson? Well, not much really. But the story goes that when Henry Hudson anchored his ship, the "Half Moon," at a New York "hook" of land, he was pleased to be greeted by Indian children. Since "kinder" is the Dutch word for children, he named the area "Kinderhook." Some time later, Van Buren was born in Kinderhook and became famous when he rose from potboy at a tavern to president of the USA! That's when he got the nickname "Old Kinderhook," which was later shortened to O.K. His supporters used this to try to convince voters he was an O.K. or good guy but the use of O.K. spread to indicate any kind of approval or agreement. Soon it became one of the best-known American slang expressions and was recognized internationally. H.L. Mencken once called it "the most shining and successful Americanism ever invented." So that's how Hudson and Van Buren became strangely connected—OK?

Did you ever know anyone with a nickname that stuck? A great-grandma still being called Whoopsie or Bitsy? A great-granddad still addressed as Izzy or even Junior? Sometimes it's hard in a conversation for seniors to remember names of movie stars or sports heroes or even long-time friends with regular names but we often have quick recall for the Whoopsies and Izzys. And the Old Kinderhooks.

Dear Lord, although seniors get the bad rap of being forgetful, we are the ones who recall the values and morals of our youth. And we know that our background and circumstances may have influenced us but whether we came from a small town or a bustling city, from a menial job like Van Buren had or a prestigious college diploma, it's where we are now and where we might still go tomorrow that matters. OK?

kite

A kite is a toy, a thing of beauty, a way to fly without wings. It's also a word used in a funny expression. When someone wants you to "get lost," they might say, "Aww, go fly a kite!" Actually, they'd be telling you to go do something nice because kite-flying can be fun. But did you know that same expression used in Spain could be "Go fly an asparagus!" Isn't that a funny idea? An asparagus is a funny-looking vegetable that is hard to describe, just like a kite is hard to describe. You almost have to SEE one to understand what it is. A kite can be lots of different shapes and sizes and colors but ALL kites have a looong string so you can take the kite outside on a windy day, run with it, hold on to the string until the air catches the kite and it soars into the sky while you stand on the ground wishing you could fly like the kite. Of course, most people reach an age when they are just as happy to stand on the ground and watch someone else running and flying the kite. But even then, it's an awesome experience.

Dear Lord, thank you for the wonderful gift of wind, for the breeze that can cool my face on a hot summer day or make a kite fly high into the sky. But, Lord, even if I ever get to go to Spain, even on the windiest day, I don't think I will try to fly an asparagus.

knick-knack

A knick-knack is a thing that is more ornamental than useful, a thing that might look nice sitting around the house but doesn't DO anything. It's a doodad, a whatchamacallit, a bauble, a VALUABLE piece of junk. But you love it and that makes it valuable. It can be fun to collect knick-knacks even if they don't DO anything, and the older you grow, the more you may collect. The world is full of things that WORK—refrigerators, lamps, cars, dishwashers, televisions. They're workers. But it can be fun to have un-workers too. Do you have any knick-knacks in your house or your office—or maybe even in your yard? Why do you like them even if they don't DO anything? Maybe it's the same reason God loves you even on the days you don't DO anything—because you're special to him. Now isn't that a wonderful thing to know?

Dear Lord, I confess. I have way too many doodads in my house. Someday I'm going to dust them all and sell them at a garage sale. But not yet, Lord, not yet.

knot

A knot is something you tie in a thread or a rope or the ribbon on a birthday present. There are lots of ways to tie a knot and some knots even have special names according to the way they are tied. Those names include thief knot, granny knot, clove hitch, cat's-paw, sheepshank, rolling hitch, outside clinch, and Englishman's tie. Then when people get married, they call it "tying the knot," when people are very nervous or worried, they might get a "knot in the stomach" and when you get in a lot of trouble, you have a "knotty" problem. If you ever get "all tied up" so you're too busy to do your chores at home or say your prayers at night or help a neighbor or just sit down and have a good giggle, you better do something to get yourself UNtied. Being all tied up in a knot is KNOT a good way to spend a life.

Dear Lord, today's television news programs show us ALL the world's troubles and when we add them to our own personal worry list, it can be overwhelming. We could spend all day every day just tying knots in our psyches. It doesn't matter whether we know how to tie a sheepshank or a rolling hitch, what we need to do is spend more time using that knotted string that is known as a rosary! That's a good way to meditate, spend some quiet time, and pray to learn how to turn some of those knotty problems of ours over to you, Lord.

knuckle

A knuckle is the place where your finger bends when you make a fist. Knuckle Ball is something a baseball pitcher throws; knucklehead might be someone who doesn't know how to throw a knuckle ball; knuckle sandwich is what you get when a guy hits you in the mouth with his fist because you called him a knucklehead! So you have to be careful before you call someone a knucklehead and once you do, you have to be careful to know when not to knuckle under. Now you probably knew all that but it's a good reminder to see where things could lead once you bend your fingers to make a fist!

Maybe the kids in your family or your neighborhood have never heard of a knuckle sandwich but they DO need to know how important it is to stand up for what you know is wrong and what is right. Someone needs to tell them that when you KNOW you're right about something important (like not using drugs or cheating or stealing) then you shouldn't knuckle under just because some knucklehead tries to get you to do something stupid. Someone needs to tell them that. Could that someone be you?

> *Dear Lord, today's kids are bombarded with mixed signals, with enticements, entrapments, with invitations to accept wrong as right, with violence much worse than knuckle sandwiches, and sometimes they need to hear a gentle reminder of the "other side" from someone they trust, someone who cares about them. Please give seniors the courage to speak out—but with open hands, not fists.*

law

Law is a rule, a principle, a formula, a commandment. Laws are necessary—in business, in government, at home, at work, on the highway, even in the neighborhood. But some of the OLD laws sound funny to us now. Did you know that at one time it was against the law to take a bath more than once a month? And it was illegal to build a fire under a mule or to ride on a streetcar after you ate garlic! Those laws seem silly now but all of them were probably passed for good reasons. Most families have laws that were made for good reasons too. Sometimes those laws change because situations change but sometimes they DON'T change even though some family members wish they would. Do you know which set of laws has NOT changed for hundreds and hundreds of years? Well, of course you know. It's the Ten Commandments. You can probably recite them from memory. And maybe you even know all the words to "The Star Spangled Banner." You are a law-abiding citizen—unless you've taken more than one bath this month.

Dear Lord, thanks for giving us guidelines that can point the way to a good life. Lawsy mercy, what would we do without them?

library

My first definition for this word would be: One of my favorite places, full of mystery and romance, history and nuance, fact and fiction. But the library has an amazing history of its own. The first "known" library was a collection of clay tablets in ancient Babylonia. The first private library in ancient Greece was probably that of Aristotle. Euripides and Plato also had large libraries and later Mark Antony is reputed to have given the vast 200,000-volume library of the kings of Pergamum as a gift to Cleopatra! The earliest public library still existing today is the Vatican Library in Rome, founded in 1450. And in America, a public library was opened in Boston as early as 1653.

But there's more. When the original holdings of the national library in Washington, D.C., were destroyed by fire in 1814, the purchase of Thomas Jefferson's personal library of 6,457 books formed the central portion of the U.S. Library of Congress, which is now the world's largest library with over 100 million items and seven million books. And, on a personal level, a library can be a free "vacation destination" for retired folks who have the time to rest and read, find out about new authors, learn fascinating facts, and just have fun discovering the world that awaits in every book in every public library.

Dear Lord, I just learned that, by law, the library on Capitol Hill must be given two copies of every book registered for copyright in the United States—so at least seventy of my books might be in that elite company on Capitol Hill. Who knew!

license

A license is a "permit, a tag, a document that proves you have been given permission to act." Today you need a license to drive a car, to get married, to build a house, to start a business. You can't even own a dog without having a license tag to hang on his collar.

And of course, even if you have a driver's license, your car also has to have a license PLATE. And that's where the fun comes in. In recent years, people have been inventive about finding things to put on their license plates, so almost every time you drive your car you can get a chuckle out of someone else's cleverness.

And it's not always bad news that you NEED all those licenses. Whenever you have to deal with someone—a doctor, lawyer, cabdriver, plumber—you feel much safer if you know they were responsible enough to get a license. For seniors who grew up when things were a little less "organized" and didn't require so many permits or endless pages of paper trails, requiring so many licenses might seem like a lot of trouble but at least you don't have to keep them hung from your neck like your dog does!

Dear Lord, there's even such a thing as "poetic license." It's defined as a "deviation from fact, form, or rule used by an artist or writer for the sake of the effect gained." Now Lord, you may have noticed that I have deviated from fact, form, or rule in a few places in this book. So I hope you—and the readers—wont ask to see my license!

list

A list can be the names of people who belong to a certain club, a voting list at an election, an invitation list for a party, a price list, a checklist—or a little piece of paper you left at home on the kitchen table. You know the one I mean—the list you spent all morning making so you would remember which groceries you needed and which errands you wanted to squeeze in right after you leave the morning meeting. Today when everyone is supposed to be multi-tasking, a list helps you know where to go when and what to do when you get there. And when you reach the over-65 group, a list is almost a necessity. You should never leave home without one because it's really hard to make it through a day when you are feeling list-less.

Dear Lord, I have made lists most of my life since I have always been a multi-tasker. I have to write down all my little to-dos—bank, cleaners, library, post office, grocery—so I can have the satisfaction of checking off the ones I get done. And, Lord, I know there's one thing on my list that I don't get checked off as much as I should—studying the Bible.

lithosphere

This is a fancy word for the earth's crust, the rocky outer part of the planet which is considered to be about fifty miles in thickness. That's a bit thicker than the crust on the pie Great Aunt Sue brought for Thanksgiving! But crusty is a word that is also sometimes used to describe certain senior citizens. They have opinions set in thick rock, never to be changed. And they probably think it's a compliment to be called "crusty." But seriously, folks, opinions need to be taken out and aired every fifty years or so. The airplane and the computer and even ice-makers and electric cars are probably here to stay even if some seniors think they are too farfetched to catch on. So if you are one of the crusty ones, scrub up your own lithosphere and save your strength for holding on to serious things like rock-hard morals, ethics, and even basic civility—all of which seem to be in dire danger these days.

Dear Lord, Some crusty characters, no matter what their age, can be fun to know—but not always to live with. Help us all to know when to hold tight and when it's time for a change.

mail

Mail includes letters, boxes, and packages that are delivered from one place to another by the post office. Years ago, there was only the pony express and men rode ponies from city to city, post office to post office, to deliver mail. Eventually, that grew into an elaborate postal service using buses, trains, trucks, and airplanes to take mail across town or across the world. But you have to pay for this service. Before 1863, the postal service in the United States was FREE. Today it can be costly to mail a bunch of Christmas or birthday gifts to out-of-town friends or family. BUT sending an important letter or a birthday card across the country for just a few cents still seems like a bargain.

And NOW most people have e-mail which you can send from your home computer and maybe get an answer back in just a few minutes. And there's texting and Twitter and all kinds of new options for communication. Yet, once the ponies went out of business, you had to start paying, in one way or another. Mail is no longer free. In fact, do you know anything that is free today? Think about it. Well, the air you breathe, the sunshine that warms you, the breeze that cools you, the wildflowers in the forest, and joy and laughter are all still FREE. You don't even need a buy-one-get-one-free coupon! So help yourself to something FREE today.

Dear Lord, some people love coupons and most people love free. In today's economy, coupons can help with a large grocery bill and free is always welcome, unless there are strings attached. Thank you for the past gen-

erations who were always putting aside a bit for tomor-row and please help the newer generations who seem to spend now, worry later. Teach us all to value the free gifts you give us every day.

mask

There's a gas mask, a Halloween mask, a fancy masquerade mask, and masking tape (which can fix a lot of things but unfortunately cannot be used to mask wrinkles). And then there's the invisible mask that some people wear to conceal their true feelings or even their true character or intentions. Do you ever wear that kind of mask? When someone hurts your feelings, or when you are disappointed or unhappily surprised, do you put on your devil-may-care mask and try to laugh it off? When your point of view or your religious faith or your knowledge in a certain area comes under attack and you feel you must defend yourself, do you put on your invulnerable mask even though you might rather run away or say "whatever"? When you are waiting for a medical diagnosis, do you wear your brave mask even though you may be shaking in your boots?

During a long life, people may need to wear different masks in a career or a home situation. And as you get older, you may feel less confident and think you need to take out a mask sometimes OR you may be sick of masking your true feelings and just tell it like it is. OR you might become an "observer" and start to figure out which kind of masks your friends and acquaintances are wearing! Let the game begin!

Dear Lord, sometimes it seems life IS a masquerade. We often wear a mask trying to keep from hurting others—and may end up hurting ourselves. So help us to use our senior "wisdom" to know when to mask or unmask. And, Lord, sometimes I even want to wear a mask with you when I want to pretend that I'm right and everybody else is wrong. But I know it won't work since you can see right through me. Oh well.

medicine

Medicine is a concoction made to cure an illness or to make you feel better. It often helps an upset stomach, a cough, a drippy nose, a sore toe—and many serious life-threatening ailments. Some seniors are all too familiar with this word and have a fistful of prescriptions to prove it.

But did you know some people think the best medicine is CHOCOLATE? No matter how bad they feel, just a bit of chocolate can make them feel much better. Once there was an Aztec ruler named Montezuma and evidently he did not stop at just a bit. It has been reported that the officials and people who lived in his palace drank TWO THOUSAND pitchers of chocolate every day!

There is no report about whether this cured anything but it must have made them all feel better. Does chocolate make you feel better? If it does, stop everything and eat a chocolate bar right now. OR do you know someone who is sick or sad or just feels bad and needs something to feel better? Send or take that person some chocolate as soon as possible!

Dear Lord, there's a song that says, "just a spoonful of sugar helps the medicine go down," and today they say that dark chocolate is very good for your health. So thank you, Lord, for the first people who figured out how to grind cacao beans and add a few spoonfuls of sugar and keep changing the mixture until they came up with candy and cakes and cookies and hot chocolate to drink on a cold winter night. Thank you for this delicious way to make many people feel much better.

microscope

A microscope is an instrument of lenses that magnify so you can get a better look at something too small to be examined by the human eye—a drop of water, a tiny bug, the amount left in your checking account or the small print on your medicine bottle. Did you know that people began using glass lenses to see better waaay back in the 1300s? About 300 years later, a Dutch family, the Janssens, tried putting one lens over another in a tube and invented the compound microscope. Then another Dutchman, named Anton Van Leeuwenhoek, started using microscopes to study bacteria and found how useful this tool could be in scientific study. Since then, the use of microscopes has helped make important discoveries in science, medicine, and biology.

It's amazing how things look when they are magnified and seen "up close." Even the wing of a fly or the petal of a flower have special designs you'd never see at a glance. Have you noticed how some people are like that too? You have to look at them very closely and get to know them "up close" before you realize how special they are. So if you need to wear specs, wear them proudly so you can get a better look at all the special things and special people in your world.

Dear Lord, thank you for inventors and microscopes and amazing scientific discoveries. And, Lord, remind me to be careful to look "up close" at all the people YOU invented.

molecule

A molecule is a minute particle, a teeny-tiny bit of something. For instance, the air you breathe is made up of molecules that are always changing as the wind blows, the earth turns, the sun goes down, and the moon comes up! Since nature continually recycles the air, some SAY that WE may be breathing some of the same molecules of air once breathed by Michelangelo, Thomas Edison, or maybe even Jesus! Isn't that an interesting idea? Most people take the air they breathe for granted—until they get a delicious whiff of a neighbor's bar-b-q or the flowery scent of perfume when a snazzy lady passes by. Maybe we should think about all the molecules God used to make everything in the world, even the air we breathe. If we do that, every breath we take can be a prayer of gratitude.

AHHH!

Dear Lord, you thought of everything, didn't you—the trees, the flowers, the mountains and the valleys, the animals and the people AND the air we all need to survive. The doctor always says, "Breathe in, breathe out," but as we do that every day, we should not take those molecules of air for granted. Once in a while, we should maybe think about whose molecule of air we would most like to be breathing?

napkin

Napkin is a small piece of paper or cloth that you use to wipe your messy mouth or sticky fingers when you're having a meal or a snack. But did you know napkins were once the size of towels? Back before forks and knives were invented, people ate huge meals using only their fingers so they NEEDED towels to wipe their hands. Some rich folks also used "finger bowls"— bowls filled with flower-scented water—so they could wash their hands before they left the table. And did you know that at one time napkins were also used like "doggy bags"? When a banquet ended, guests would wipe their hands and then wrap up leftovers in the napkins to take home. And it was considered bad manners to leave without your napkin!

The word "napkin" comes from a French word that meant "little tablecloth." The British used this word to describe a large cloth which they tied around the waist like an apron—so they could protect their clothes while they ate and also have a place to wipe their hands. So, through the years, a napkin has been a towel, a tablecloth, and an apron! Some seniors are familiar with all three. When you enjoy a nice meal, you might prefer a towel-size or regular-size napkin but please don't wipe your fingers on the tablecloth!

Dear Lord, today most people are polite enough to use napkins and most are blessed enough to have food but there are still so many who have neither. And many of them are senior citizens who have little hope of things getting better. Help us, Lord, to be alert to look out for those who have less than we do, to give thanks for what we have and to share as much as we can.

neon

Neon is the gas used to make the brilliantly colored signs you often see burning brightly above restaurants, gas stations, stores, etc. Strangely enough, neon itself is colorless! But some scientists discovered that when you put neon in a tube and pass electricity through it, it glows with a bright red/orange color. Later they added mercury vapors to the neon and got MORE colors. And today those tubes are shaped to form all kinds of glowing neon letters and designs.

You may have noticed that some people (especially those of an advanced age!) sometimes seem colorless and boring like colorless neon, but they can change when something is added—something like kindness, friendship, compassion, or a helping hand. Of course, people of all ages can seem colorless or boring until you get to know them, but seniors seem to get labeled more quickly. So if you have some friends who need a bit of glowing, see if you can help. Take 'em to lunch at one of those places with a big neon sign shouting "Good Eats."

Dear Lord, sometimes I sit in a mall or an airport or even at church and see people who seem to have lost spirit. The color has drained from their face, the sparkle from their eyes. Please send them help, Lord. Send something or someone who can turn on a neon light in their brain screaming, "Wake up! God loves you."

nictitate

Nictitate has nothing to do with nicking a tater or sending an e-mail from Nick to Tate. Nope. This fun word simply means WINK! Yes, it does. No joke. When you nictitate, you wink or blink. Some birds wink and blink faster than you can count. Some people wink when they are making a joke or trying to get your attention. Look out the window today and wink both eyes as fast as you can. You will see the world moving just like it does in those old black-and-white movies—in a funny, jiggly way. Then close both eyes and then open them quickly and pretend you are an Alien who has just landed on earth. You have never seen anything like this on YOUR planet. You've never seen such colors or shapes or plants or people.

Everything you touch or taste or smell or hear today will be brand new. As an alien, you are discovering this fascinating planet called EARTH. If anyone asks what you're doing, just

wink and tell them you've found a really silly way to turn an ordinary day into a fun time—without spending any money or going anywhere!

Dear Lord, a wise person once said, "The best thing great teachers can do for us is to help us discover what is already present." We're never too old to learn a lesson like that. Lord, you put so many wonders on our planet and all we have to do is to keep our eyes open and be willing to discover them.

nightshade

Nightshade is not a shade you pull down at night. It's a family of flowering plants. And it's a very strange family. It includes herbs, shrubs, trees, flowers, fruits, and important crop plants like the potato and the eggplant, yet one type of this plant is known as the DEADLY nightshade because it's poison. Another variety is known as the stinking nightshade. You can guess why.

Isn't it strange how some plants can be related to one another and yet are SO different? Have you noticed how, like plants, some human families are like that too? Those in the same family can look, talk, and behave very differently. Some might like sports, some arts and crafts, some travel the world while others hardly ever leave home. And that's what makes families so interesting. Each member is similar but unique in likes and dislikes.

In spite of that, society often puts people into groups—"Oh, he's from the wrong side of town so he's probably no good," "She's a teenager and all teenagers are troublesome." And that's a DEADLY way to judge people, including senior citizens. Once you reach a certain age, some people label you "old" and tend to treat you differently. Of course, sometimes they treat you better, offering you help, carrying your packages, inviting you to lunch. Yes, age has problems but a few perks too. So enjoy those and remember, no matter how many birthday candles you've lit, you are not just old. You are still you, uniquely made by God.

Dear Lord, thank you for making plants, pets, and people all so different. Life would be deadly boring if they were all exactly alike. So help us, Lord, to not judge too quickly—and to be grateful for every candle on the cake. They cast a lovely light.

norm

Norm could be a man's name—short for Norman. OR it could mean average, typical, or conforming to a type, standard, or pattern. It could be an idea of the way people in a certain group are expected to look, think, or act. If you follow the "norm," you are normal or just like all the other people. BUT if you look or think or act in a different way, this does NOT mean that you are NOT normal. It just means that you are YOU. For example, did you know a giraffe has seven bones in his looong neck, exactly the same number of bones a mouse has in his neck? The giraffe's neck does not look like the mouse's neck. Both

WEIRD, HUH?

are normal but both are different. In the same way, just because you have reached a certain age, you do not have to look, think, or act exactly like others who are the same age. You are still YOU, just the way God made you.

Dear Lord, I was just reading something that would NORMALLY be for children but I like it. It's a line from a Dr. Seuss book: "Be who you are and say what you feel, because those who mind don't matter and those who matter don't mind."

oesophagus

Did you ever see an oesophagus? Do you ever hope to see one? Well, don't count on it. The famous writer, Mark Twain, once wrote of a morning in October: "The larch and the pomegranate flung their purple and yellow flames in brilliant splashes along the slanting sweep of the woodland; the sensuous fragrance of innumerable deciduous flowers rose upon the swooning atmosphere; far in the empty sky a solitary oesophagus slept upon motionless wing; everywhere brooded stillness, serenity, and the peace of God."

The solitary bird was solitary all right because Twain had invented the bird. Actually, few readers questioned him about it but a few know-it-alls were quick to point it out.

So you won't be seeing the bird but you can find the word in a dictionary explained as the British version of esophagus. And you know you need your esophagus to swallow things just like most people swallowed Twain's imagined exotic bird name. Sometimes you have to swallow a lot of things in today's world as you seek the stillness, serenity, and peace of God.

Dear Lord, thanks to Twain's imaginative description, I too can close my eyes and picture that October morning and smell the flowers and spot the solitary bird. Thank you for the many beautiful passages we can find in books to transport us from our busy here to your beyond.

okra

Okra is a four-letter word at my house. Yes, I know it's spelled with four letters but that does not express how much my husband hates okra. I told him that okra was so valuable in ancient Angola that tribes made "sharp knife" raids into neighbors' fields to steal the vegetable, killing anyone who stood in their way. I told him the Arabs held okra to be a rare delicacy fit for weddings and other special occasions, naming it uehka, which means "a gift." He was not impressed. I even told him that in England, okra is sometimes called ladyfingers. He, who loves all things English, was not impressed. He does not want a dish of okra anywhere near his plate on the dining room table.

On the other hand, my son, who knows nothing about ancient Angola or Arab weddings, loves okra and wants it stir-fried and ON his plate any time possible. Just showsya taste does not span generations.

How do YOU feel about okra or gumbo or ladyfingers? Do you have special no-nos or yes-yeses when it comes to foods? Some seniors only want to eat things familiar to them from childhood. Others like to try lots of new recipes, enjoying the experience of new food combinations. Whatever age you are, like so many things in life, it's just a matter of taste.

Dear Lord, I grew up in the South where okra is sometimes considered gourmet. Sometimes not. Thank you, Lord, for such a variety of vegetables AND people— even the four-letter ones.

onion

Onion is a strange vegetable that can make you smile or cry. You might smile when you're enjoying a serving of meatloaf, stew, or a casserole made with lots of oniony flavor. But you might cry if you are the one who had to peel the onions to go into those recipes. Do you know why peeling an onion can make you cry? When you cut an onion, it releases a special chemical  in the air. This chemical reacts with the moisture on the surface of your eyes and forms a weak solution of sulfuric ACID! What? Yes. But wait! When the acid starts to sting, your eyes fight back! They quickly produce tears to dilute the acid and wash it away. Isn't it amazing how God made your body so it will react to danger and fight back to try to protect you? Of course, some seniors might feel that their body has let them down by failing here or there or allowing aches to find places to settle in and pitch a tent. Well, maybe you have also let your body down at times by not taking good care of it. So the next time you peel an onion, show your body you care. Put on some swim goggles to keep that acid out. It might get a laugh—which is always good for a body.

Dear Lord, Thank you for making such swimmingly sensational things as onions and eyes. Thank you for making body parts that fight back against intruders.

And remind us to do our part in taking care of all these good things you made for us.

opsimathy

If you've never heard this word before, don't look for it in your dictionary because I doubt it will be there. It's not listed in mine. But I was thumbing through an old thesaurus and there it was, under "learning." Opsimathy is defined as "education late in life." Wow! Since it's too late for me to get more education early in life, I was delighted to find that education late in life is not only possible but there is even a word for it! So what kind of education would YOU like to seek? Would you like to enroll in some classes at a nearby community college? Join a chorus and learn how to sing better? Take lessons to learn how to play guitar? Take an educational televison course? Join a Scripture study group?

Volunteer to be a theater usher so you could see all the new plays free and get educated about the theatuh? Volunteer at an art museum and learn about the arts? Or have lunch with your or someone else's teenage grandchildren and get educated in a very different current lifestyle? See? There are all kinds of ways for OPSIMATHY to become a part of your life!

Dear Lord, there's an old saying about how you are never too old to learn something new. Well, there are so many things going on here and there that I learn something new almost every day. And today I learned the definition of opsimathy. So now I can take the rest of the day off and have a cup of tea. Would you care to join me?

owl

Owl is the name for a big bird that keeps asking, "WHO? WHO?" That's a bit like children who keep asking, "WHY? WHY?" And the way some senior citizens keep asking, "WHAT? WHAT did you say?"

Yes, some senior citizens are hear-ably challenged. And it is not a laughing matter. It's embarrassing and frustrating to have to wonder what other people are saying. Too bad we don't all have owl ears. The barn owl not only has telescopic vision but a superb sense of hearing that helps him hunt at night in total darkness. Most of us only need to hunt in total darkness when the electricity goes out and we can't remember where we left a flashlight, so I guess God knew we wouldn't ordinarily need owl ears.

But hearing is a sensitive subject. The owl's ears are so sensitive that they are surrounded by small feathered flaps that can be closed over the delicate inner parts of the ear when there is TOO MUCH noise. Seniors who have no hearing problems might like to have some of those flaps although furry flaps could clash with earrings. Guess God knew that too.

Dear Lord, please help seniors with hearing problems and help all of us to pay closer attention and truly listen to family and friends—just in case they're trying to tell us something important. And Lord, help us listen more closely to you too. Whenever you talk to us it is always something important.

paper clip

The paper clip is a piece of wire or plastic twisted into flat loops that can be used to hold several pieces of paper together so they won't get lost or blow away or fall into your soup. It was invented a long time ago (in 1919), so it makes one wonder what people used to keep their papers together before the clip. Maybe they used fancy paperweights. Or maybe they rolled the papers up and tied them with a string. Do you ever feel weighted down or all strung out? Have a day when you just can't get it all together? Maybe somebody said something to you or about you that wasn't nice and you feel bad or sad. Maybe you had plans to go somewhere but the plans got cancelled at the last minute and you're disappointed. Maybe you have so many chores to do you think you'll never get them all finished and life is not fair. Well, I know it sounds silly but just PRETEND you are making a list of all your terrible problems and then you are paper-clipping them together and tossing them into the trash or sending them into orbit. Now! Since you won't have to spend all day worrying about those problems, you should have enough extra time to get those chores finished. OR you could pretend you're on a cruise in the Caribbean and just take a nap in the sunshine!

Dear Lord, thank you for inventing people who invent handy things like paper clips, and thank you for the gift of imagination so we can use it to cruise or to come visit you for a chat.

peanut butter

Peanut butter is a gooey brown paste made by grinding peanuts together. It looks kinda yucky but tastes yummy. It sticks to bread and sometimes it sticks to the roof of your mouth and it might stick to your ribs too since it's supposed to be nutritious. A lot of seniors who live alone often fall back on a PBJ for lunch when nothing in the fridge looks good. And if there are grandkids around, you must always have a jar of peanut butter on the shelf for emergencies. For this handy snack you can thank George Washington Carver, the man who discovered lots of ways to use peanuts, sweet potatoes, and soybeans. You probably know that he was born into a black slave family around the time of the Civil War and grew up to become an agricultural chemist. His research led to ways of improving crops and making synthetic products out of things like potatoes and wood. His many innovations helped improve the economy of the South and he became a real hero of science. You wouldn't think studying a peanut could make you a hero, would you? But it did! So why don't you become a scientist today? Look around and find some little ORDINARY thing to study or think about—a sugar bowl, a notepad, a picture frame, a deck of cards. Make a list of all the good things this one little ordinary thing has brought into your life. And learn to appreciate all things, great and small.

Dear Lord, the word "peanut" is often used to describe a small person or a trifling amount but Carver looked at a peanut and saw possibilities. Today peanuts are even used in soaps, pharmaceutical preparations, and cosmetics. So teach us, Lord, to sometimes think small!

perihelion

This is the point in the orbit of a planet or comet when it is NEAREST the Sun. The APHELION is when it is FARTHEST from the Sun. Since the Earth travels in an oval rather than a circle around the Sun, it is sometimes farther and sometimes closer. BUT when it is the closest, at its Perihelion, the Sun is still 91,400,000 miles away from earth. Did you ever sunbathe by a pool and feel like you were very near the sun? No matter how hot you got, you were still at least 91,400,000 miles away! And that's about how far away some seniors feel from today's technological, anything-goes, commandment-challenged society. Instead of retiring, they are expected to always be adapting, to know how to cope with e-mail, i-pods, ATMs, texts, Tweets, outer space, inner space, and strange words like perihelion and aphelion. Well, at least it isn't boring. So just hang in there, reaching for the warmth of the Sun and the love of the Son.

Dear Lord, in the midst of this ever-evolving, sometimes exciting, sometimes frightening world, on some days it's tempting to feel like you are ninety-four million miles away too since you aren't sending a burning bush or a meal of manna to help us adapt. But that's OK, Lord, on some days you might think we are far away too since you haven't heard much praying coming from this frightening world. Sorry about that, Lord. Mea culpa. Mea culpa.

pig

A pig is a young swine, an oinker, but also a surprisingly smart animal that has been very useful to people for a very long time. Archaeologists say there were tame pigs in China over six thousand years ago! Historians say that Hernando de Soto brought the first pigs to America when he landed in Florida in 1539. Scientists say pigs have been very useful in the field of medicine because they were used in experiments on diabetes, alcoholism, and heart disease. So it seems the lowly pig has been a BIG help to society in lots of ways but have you ever seen someone insult someone else by calling him or her a pig?

Unfortunately, people have often found ways to insult each other by comparing people to animals—dumb as an ox, slow as a snail, sly as a fox, fat as a cow. And there are plenty of insults or jokes made about senior citizens too. You've probably heard them all. Some people use words like geezer, prehistoric, obsolete, out-of-date, in one's dotage, senile, decrepit, fossil— well, you get the picture but fuggedaboutit. There are lots of words about age that are complimentary—venerable, time-honored, wise, discerning, perceptive, understanding, patient, or lovable. And remember, today the word "antique" describes something very valuable.

> *Dear Lord, it's so easy to find fault, make fun of some-one, point out their deficiencies instead of their good qualities. So many elders have been mentors and good examples for youth. Some have jovial personalities that show others how to sometimes laugh when the world does not laugh with you. Please, Lord, help society to keep seeing how these antiques are very valuable.*

"YOU'RE SUCH A PERSON"

pomegranate

Recently, pomegranates have become stars. After years of quietly staying in the background, this wrinkly red fruit now appears regularly in supermarket produce sections, and pomegranate juice can be found in the ingredient listing of an amazing variety of foods. But do you know what a pomegranate has to do with Christianity? Well, a pomegranate is about the size of a large orange and it has a red thick skin and it's full of lots and lots of seeds. And when it gets really, really ripe—or mature—on the tree, it bursts and seeds go flying in all directions. So the design of a pomegranate was used in wood carvings and decorations in many early Christian churches because it seemed to be a good symbol for Christianity—a lot of people all together in one "skin," just bursting with the Good News, ready to fly off in all directions to spread the seeds of faith. How about that! Are you mature enough now to be just bursting with the Good News and ready to fly around spreading the seeds of faith by example? Think about it.

Dear Lord, even though we cherish the faith and love your message and try to live it in our everyday life, maybe we stay quietly in the background too much. Maybe maturity should make us more outspoken about our faith, more willing to talk about it and rejoice in it. Remind us, Lord, as we ripen, to follow the example of the wrinkly red pomegranate.

purple martin

You've probably seen some bird houses in the neighborhood that provide housing for this strange but helpful bird. The purple martin is not really purple—but it IS a dragon killer! The male martin might look a bit purple but it's actually more of a blue-black color and the female is gray. But they are both helpful because they LIKE to eat mosquitoes, flies, and wasps and their FAVORITE food is DRAGONFLIES! Imagine! Little birds that slay dragons.

Some elders find a lot of dragons in their senior years and they feel like they just don't have the strength to be a dragon-slayer any more. They've spent their whole life fighting their own battles so it's hard to ask for help, but sometimes it becomes necessary. And maybe that's good. Like an old song said, "Everybody needs somebody sometime." Asking for or accepting help gives someone else a chance to be useful. So when too many dragons come charging into your life, don't give up but DO give in. Let someone else have a chance to be a hero, a helper, a care-giver, a dragon slayer. Who knows? Maybe some of those helpers might be guardian angels sent by Someone who cares for you very much.

Dear Lord, some people are just natural born do-ers and when they get to an age where they need help, it's so hard for them to face that fact. Help them, Lord. Help them see that independence is a good and wonderful thing but dependence is important too. We all depend on you, Lord, but sometimes we just gotta have a human helping hand to join us in the fight against those senior dragons.

quartz

Quartz is a mineral that has been used in various ways like in a quartz heater and a quartz-iodine lamp (whatever that is) but today the most well-known use is in a quartz watch—to eliminate the tick-tock! Way back in 1880, a scientist discovered that if you cut quartz a certain way and then pass electricity through it, the quartz will move back and forth at a constant rate. In the 1920s, smart clockmakers got the idea they could use quartz this way to replace the machinery in a clock that went back and forth and made the sound of tick-tock. Without the tick-tock, they could make a SILENT clock. And after the microchip was invented, it was possible to use this technique in small wrist watches, so now you can have accurate and QUIET time wherever you go—without a tick or a tock.

Imagine what it must have been like before clocks and watches were invented. You would never know if you were going to be late or early but it wouldn't matter because nobody else knew either! Now you have no excuse because there are

"YOU'RE LATE"

clocks and watches everywhere. Since you can always know what time it is now, see if you can spend ten minutes of time today without making a sound.

Without making a sound, what will you do, what will you think, what will you plan, or maybe what will you pray?

Dear Lord, it may sound easy to not make a sound—but it isn't easy. I've tried it. No matter how old you are, whatever you do, it makes a sound—even wriggling around in your chair. You have to close your eyes, relax, welcome the silence, quiet your psyche, and think, imagine, welcome whatever quirky thoughts come into your head...accept, experience, appreciate.

question

A question is an inquiry, something you ask to get information—or sometimes just to aggravate. Some people seem to QUESTION everything you say or do. No matter what subject you bring up, they immediately question whether you know what you are talking about. No matter what you do to try to please them, they immediately find fault and question why you would want to do such a thing. What you bought was too expensive, not appropriate or useless. That can be very aggravating.

And then, they sometimes turn a conversation into an interrogation, questioning you about your friends, your plans, maybe even your personal finances. Oh my, oh my. Do you know anyone like this? Do you have to deal with anyone like this? Could you possibly ever BE someone like this? Of course not!

But back to the definition. Asking questions to get needed information about a medicine or a diagnosis or a possibility or a way to get from here to there is often necessary and important. Asking questions about a new subject that truly interests you, something you think you would like to delve into, to learn more about, now that can be an unquestionably wise thing to do.

But the next time you ask a question, first ask yourself why? Do you really need an answer or do you just hope to aggravate?

Dear Lord, children often challenge parents with the "need to know" basis to answer a question, and as they get older, parents sometimes feel the need to respond to children in the same way but, Lord, you must get more questions than anyone. Forgive us for questioning your wisdom, your commandments, your love. Give us the patience and faith to wait for you to give us the answers when we "need to know."

quilt

A quilt is a bedcover that is made by stitching together lots of little pieces of material—and usually the pieces are all different colors and fabrics and designs. Some quilts are fabulously beautiful, some are plain, some are very old, some are new, but they are all very cozy and wonderful to own. Quilts remind us of yesteryear when founding mothers met in log cabins to turn scraps of material into warmth for their families. Quilts remind us of today when new quilting machines can do the work of many hands and designers are turning

simple bedcoverings into art. But quilts also make us see how they are like a business or a family or a church—lots of individuals, some of different colors, different backgrounds and talents but all joined together to make something important. Isn't that a warm, happy thought—to be a unique, special, one-of-a-kind person and yet stitched together with lots of other one-of-a-kind persons to form a successful business or a happy family or a church that praises God who made them all?

Do you have any family heirloom quilts? If you do, cherish them. If you don't, now's a good time to start one that can become a family treasure in the future. If you're not a stitcher, you can be a shopper, going to quilt and craft shows until you find just the one that can become your family's old-new heirloom. Don't just save the quilt though. Use it, enjoy it. When you climb under it and get all cozy, you can think of family members of the past and imagine those to come in the future. You may be surprised to realize that you have been a part of many kinds of quilts—at school, at work, with friends, neigh-bors, family, and always as a part of God's world-wide quilt.

Dear Lord, I am not a stitcher, but I am sometimes a joiner, so I am thinking today of all the different quilts of which I have been a part through the years—and it's a very cozy feeling!

quit

Quit is what you do when you finish what you're doing OR when you give up. It's good to know WHEN to quit—like a tired but stubborn person who refuses to quit watching TV when it's time to quit and go to bed. Other people quit too soon like a lazy person who gets bored doing a job that needs doing and gives up without getting the job done. One kind of person who hardly ever gives up is an inventor. Inventors just keep trying ONE MORE way to do something in a new and interesting way. There have been many great and useful inventions and many not so useful. Did you know that in 1950 a patent was issued for the invention of an automatic spaghetti-spinning fork? This is NOT an invention that might change the world. But many inventions HAVE changed the world—like the electric light, the telephone, the television, and the computer. When YOU have a good idea, don't give up on it. But when you want to keep doing something but you KNOW it is time to stop, QUIT! Some seniors have this dilemna. They want everything to stay the same. Deep down, they know it is time to quit a job, to move from a large house to a more convenient place, to maybe stop driving at night or just quit complaining so much. To be happy, it is very important to know when to keep trying but also know when it is time to QUIT!

Dear Lord, sometimes it's hard to judge the difference between do more and do less. Life offers so many opportunities but also so many challenges. Sometimes sameness seems safe but it can also be just a habit that you've outgrown. Help us to know the difference, Lord.

"I QUIT!"

affle

A raffle is a lottery in which many people take chances and one person wins a nice prize. Anyone old enough to be a senior has probably taken a lot of chances on a lot of raffles. But did you know about a gentleman named Sir Stanford Raffles? He took a big chance that didn't pay off for a few years. He worked for the British East India Company and in the course of his duties, he happened to notice a swampy island called Singapore. Although it was very unattractive, he noticed that this island was at the crossroads of important trade routes for which Britain and Holland were competing. In 1819, Sir Stanford founded a British settlement in Singapore and persuaded his company to buy the island from the Sultan of Johore. Everyone in his company was not as enthusiastic about this transaction as he was and in 1826 when Raffles died, the company actually charged his widow for the expenses of the Singapore sale. BUT within a few more years, Singapore grew into a large and vitally important port and it still is today. Sadly, Raffles didn't live to see how the chance he took DID pay off and become a real "prize."

Dear Lord, senior living is always a risky business. You never know if you are going to trip over a mountain or a molehill and break something or swallow a noodle the wrong way and get all choked up. In spite of that, the fun of a raffle is the possibility that YOU might just win. So whatever age we are, it's still fun to take a chance—to take a trip to an exotic place, to move to a different house or condo, to take up a new hobby like

sky diving or rodeo riding! We must just remember—
you will never win a raffle if you never take a chance!

rag

"BUT THEY'RE COMFY!"

A rag is a piece of leftover cloth that you can use for dusting or polishing when you're cleaning house. Or it could be a raggedy or well-worn piece of clothing that eventually ends up in a rag bag where you collect scraps which could be used for making a Raggedy Ann or Andy doll while you're listening to Ragtime music and waiting for the ragout of beef and vegetables to finish simmering on the stove. You see how one thing can lead to another?

Many seniors "have rag, will travel," because they actually enjoy cleaning. Some have been accused of wearing "that old rag" again when they are sporting a favorite old-friend of an outfit. And many are good at stitching or listening to or even playing Ragtime music or stirring up delicious old recipes like ragouts. Every senior day might be a rag-bag that can start out with nothing much and end up with a lot of surprises—if you let one thing lead to another.

Dear Lord, people have teasingly called me a bag lady and a rag-picker because I am always jotting down bits and pieces of ideas on a file card or a little note and saving them for a future "something"—and they are so right. When I have enough bits and pieces, one thing leads to another and soon I have an idea for another ragtag book. So thank you, Lord, for rag dolls and rag-bags—but not for ragweed (achoo!).

railroad

Some seniors may remember when it was great fun to take a train trip or to go to the railroad station to welcome someone coming home. Although railroading is not as available now, there is one railroad that is senior-friendly because all the trains carry oxygen equipment! Actually oxygen might be needed for passengers of any age because at one point, this railroad in Peru reaches three miles high, about the same height as Mont Blanc, the tallest peak in Europe. Often called the "railroad in the sky," the trip through the towering Andes has been a great tourist at-

traction for many years. Did you ever take an exciting railroa
trip in the past that brings back pleasant memories? OR do you
have an unpleasant memory of someone trying to railroad you
into a decision you were not comfortable about? Some sales
people think seniors are an easy mark so be on guard and show
them that, with or without oxygen, seniors still know how to
stay on the right track.

> *Dear Lord, it's nice to get senior service when some-*
> *one offers to carry your packages or open a door for*
> *you but it's embarrassing sometimes when people treat*
> *seniors like kindergartners. Lord, help younger people*
> *know the difference between respect and condescension*
> *and help seniors be patient in accepting those good in-*
> *tentions. Remind us to not act so high and mighty that*
> *we might NEED some oxygen!*

rancor

Rancor is an ugly-sounding word for an ugly kind of feeling. As
you know, it means to hate or detest something—or maybe even
someone. More than just dislike, rancor is a bitter deep-seated
ill will that could cause something like the famous old Hatfield-
McCoy Feud. And you know, "them's shooting words," pardner.

It's OK to hate something evil or sinful. But sadly today the
idea of a family feud or any kind of "shooting" is not funny
any more. There are too many stories in the news of innocent
people being killed by drive-by shootings. What could have
brought our society to have such RANCOR in our midst?

FEELING A LITTLE RANCOR

Young people today are besieged on all sides with constant loud music (no place there for quiet meditation) and evil life-styles, drug-use and gang-mentality pictured as glamorous and "cool." Some of them are fortunate to turn to elders who can show them values and higher goals and offer them guidance, hope, and spirituality. But, since there are fewer "meeting grounds" for teens and the aging, thankfully, today churches and community groups are beginning to have more "intergenerational" programs where the enthusiasm of youth and the strength of seniors can combine—to help each other. And them's "winning words."

Dear Lord, with so many fractured families today, many children turn to "peers" for guidance in choosing lifestyles. It's sometimes hard for seniors to fight off rancor in dealing with teen insolence and seeming indifference from the children they have cherished so much. Help them both, Lord, the youth and the aging, to find ways to reach out to each other—by reaching out to you.

salt

Salt is something you sprinkle on food to give it more flavor. But did you know that out of every one hundred pounds of salt produced, only five pounds of it goes to the dinner table? The rest is used for a variety of things like making glass and soap, tanning leather, and melting ice off sidewalks. Salt was once VERY valuable so people were VERY careful how they used it. Today, it's so plentiful and "ordinary" that you take it for granted and never think about its value. It's one of those things that's just there—until you go on a picnic and have fresh tomatoes and NO salt because somebody forgot to bring it. Do you ever take your friends or family for granted because they're "just there"? Think about your friends and family and think about how valuable they are!

Dear Lord, we use the word salt in different ways too. Someone who is very dependable might be called "the salt of the earth." A former sailor might be called an old salt. And a "flavorful" story might be called a bit salty. But most of the time, salt just sits in its cellar, taken for granted. Forgive us, Lord, if we sometimes treat you that way too. We take you for granted because you are always there—always waiting to spice up our life if we will just pay attention and value your friendship.

squash

Squash can be the sound made when you walk in water-soaked boots. Or it can be a bug, a game, a sweetened fruit drink.

Or it can be the uncomfortable feeling you get when you are squashed in a crowded elevator OR when someone suggests serving you squash for dinner. Actually you should be very happy when you see squash on your dinner plate because a recent survey reported that if you eat squash regularly you will have a thirty-nine percent LOWER risk of dying for any cause, including heart disease and cancer! (However, eating your veggies will probably not protect you from getting squashed by a runaway ten-ton truck.)

This amazing vegetable comes in lovely autumn colors: yellow squash that could make you feel sunshiney; orange butternut squash that sounds so good (buttery and nutty both): and dark green acorn squash that seems so sturdy. So if you're worried about aging and want to live longer, and believe in surveys, start getting squashed every day!

Dear Lord, fortunately the people at my dinner table DO enjoy eating squash but they do not really believe in surveys. They DO however believe in YOU, Lord, so we just keep on getting squashed and keep on thanking you by saying a Blessing before and after every meal.

stew

Stew is a mixture that can be boring or delicious. It's made of meat and vegetables and your "secret ingredient." It could be boring like leftovers but if you add just the right amount of your secret blend of spices or whatever, it can be the family's favorite dinner. And another stew secret is that it has to cook slowly, simmering to mix in the flavors. So life is like a stew. It's made of ordinary stuff like meat and potatoes and maybe even leftover veggies but if you add some spices like friendship, lifelong learning, discovery, music, prayer, and laughter, it can be delicious. But about that slow cooking—simmering is good for stew but stewing about something is not good for life. So if some old hurt or imaginary insult has been stewing in your head too long, throw it out and start over, the way you would throw out a container of leftover stew that had been sitting in the refrigerator too long. And today look around for some new kind of "spice"—a new class or club to join or even a new park where you and a friend could maybe take a walk each day or once a week—to give you a new recipe for a more delicious life.

Dear Lord, I'm afraid stewing is a verb that is all too familiar with people of a certain age. We have had more years to add to the contents of the simmer—the hurts, the being overlooked or underpaid, the being discriminated against or unappreciated, and on and on. Help us all, Lord, to see that "a certain age" should be the time for forgiveness, not a time to just cover it up and pretend all is well but to truly face it and erase it totally—the way you, Lord, forgive us for so many failings, offenses, and shortcomings.

At different times and in different generations, success has been measured in a variety of ways. Discoveries, inventions, wealth were always considered to be successes. But in everyday life, sometimes success was measured by the size of your car or your house or your title or your income. If you had enough money to put away a little for a rainy day, you were successful. Today experts tell us that young people are not as concerned about security. They see flexibility and creativity as keys to gain professional status. And, you know, the same may be true of certain seniors. They have been told to "Reinvent yourself" and it takes flexibility and creativity to do that. Some who have been very successful in their careers have left the corporate world to pursue a totally different lifestyle. Some have left lucrative jobs to "follow their passion," to seek some kind of work they think will be more fulfilling—possibly social work, teaching, nursing, volunteering, writing, painting. One lady became a "nanny" and loved it. One man became a limo driver and enjoyed being a part of festive occasions. Many chose to spend more time with their families or to pursue spiritual development. Many have retired early so they could travel and learn what the other side of the world is like. If you could afford to reinvent yourself, what would you choose?

Dear Lord, you are the master of invention so you must be surprised at the ways your children choose to spend the days of their lives. You must have been disappointed at the way some of them have measured success. Guide us all, Lord, as we are "reinventing" so we will at least go from OK to better, instead of from bad to worse.

tax

Tax is your money that you have to give away whether you want to or not. Depending on where you live, you might pay income tax, real-estate tax, property tax, sales tax, and so on—and this can become a very "taxing" problem! Back in the days of the Romans, there was one thing that was not taxed—cemetery land. So the famous poet Virgil came up with a "burial plot" to avoid paying tax on his home. He found a dead fly and held an elaborate FLY FUNERAL. He invited friends to come and they all made speeches about the fly. Then he buried the fly in his yard, served his guests a funeral meal, and claimed he did not have to pay tax on his home because it was a cemetery! (You probably should not try this at home. The IRS does not seem to have a sense of humor.)

Most people HATE to pay taxes but they also realize that it's necessary for the people of any country to support their government—and your taxes DO help to keep the government running. So once in a while, especially in the month of April, say a little prayer for your government and all the people who work in the tax department. They have a hard job!

Dear Lord, they say there is nothing certain in life except death and taxes—and sometimes we all tax our heads worrying about both. It may be hard to have faith that our government will use our taxes wisely but we do believe in your promise, Lord, that the faithful will rest in peace.

time

Time is a special gift and every person—rich or poor, old or young, whatever race or religion or nationality—is given the same number of seconds, minutes, and hours in each day. But each one USES that time differently. And once used, time can never be bought back again. Time used in pouting, complaining, or being bored is wasted and gone forever. Time used in laughing, enjoying, doing worthwhile work, helping someone else, or learning something new is gone forever too—but you have memories and accomplishments you BOUGHT with that time. You didn't just throw it away and have nothing to show for it.

How do you use your time today? How do you plan to use it in the future? Will you treasure and appreciate every precious minute? Well, of course you won't. Who does—until they start running out of time. Maybe you should spend some time today thinking about TIME.

Dear Lord, not just on New Year's Day but on many wasted days, I firmly resolve to use time more carefully. I start out the door to get to a meeting early but I see the snow and stop to put out some food for the birds, then I notice the garbage man has come so I pull the empty cans into the garage, and that reminds me

I meant to put some mail in the box. Well, Lord, yo.
can see why I do not always get where I planned to go
when I expected to get there. I must focus more and
stop trying to squeeze too many things in at once. But,
Lord, you know that my time is your time and you are
still with me before and after and on the way. Thanks.

trap

This word can entrap you with all the places you find it—in a
golf sand trap, a plumbing "trap," a police trap, a trapdoor—
but one of the most popular ones is a mouse trap. And thereby
hangs a tale (or tail!) From 1690 to the 1980s, there was a little
jewelry shop tucked away in a corner in London and its name
was the Silver Mousetrap. This strange name dates back to a
time when rich fashionable women had strange hairdos. They
would spend a day or two having their hair turned into a huge
extraordinary sculpture! First the long hair would be piled as
high as possible, often with the addition of some artificial hair,
and then plaster birds might be added to make it look like the
birds were nesting in the hair or maybe a small ship to sail
on the waves. And to make all this stay in place, the hair was
stiffened with flour, chalk dust, or arsenic powder. And you
thought you knew about a bad hair day!

These creations took so long to make they had to be slept
with for weeks at a time and of course the hair could not be
washed. Since rich ladies lived in huge mansions or even cas-
tles, mice lived there too and they often found a head of piled-
up hair a fine place to scurry in and out of at night. So the little

jewelry store began to make little ladylike silver mousetraps which could be placed strategically about the head at bed-time—to help ladies who had nightmice instead of nightmares!

This long story is just to give you a laugh about hair since aging often thins hair so your hairdo won't "do" right any more—and that's not a laughing matter! So if you have this elder problem, just be glad you don't have to sleep with mouse-traps on your pillow.

> *Dear Lord, there have always been many kinds of "traps" in life and now it seems even more so in our technocratic society, but the 1600s sound even worse. At least today, we can "style" our thinning locks with a bit of hair spray instead of flour, chalk, or arsenic powder!*

uh-oh

Someone once said that this is the most terrifying phrase in the English language. You might say it when you're trying a new recipe and you suddenly notice you were supposed to stir in one TEAspoon of salt, not one TABLEspoon. You might say it when the car in front of you suddenly stops but you don't. And, even worse, when a dentist looks at your X-rays and says "uh-oh," you know it might mean another million-dollar tooth repair. Well, life is full of uh-oh moments but you usually manage to find a solution, work it out, and get on with life without dwelling on it too long. If you have learned to deal with the uh-ohs, then you are eligible to say the happier phrase, "ah-hah!"

Dear Lord, too many people get stuck in the "uh-oh phrase" phase of life and start to expect everything to go wrong and nothing to ever be right again. Please help them get unstuck so they can enjoy the great victorious feeling of handling small emergencies so they can experience the "ah-hah phrase" phase of life.

umbrella

Umbrella is a funny-sounding name for something that looks like an upside-down saucer with a handle on it—which you hold over your head when it rains. Actually, that sounds like a silly thing to do, standing outside in the rain with an upside-down saucer over your head! But did you know the umbrella was first used 3400 years ago in Mesopotamia, a desert land where it almost NEVER rained? And that's how it got its funny name. The name umbrella comes from the Latin word that means "shade" because the FIRST umbrellas were used to protect Mesopotamians from the harsh desert SUN. The umbrella was used for years primarily to shade the person who carried it—and some "important people" even employed servants to carry the umbrella over them. Finally, Roman women got the idea to cover their paper sunshades with some kind of oil that made the umbrellas stiff enough to protect them from the rain too. Since then, the umbrella has been used by everyone and anyone who is "too dumb to come in out of the rain."

Actually it's not dumb to enjoy the rain—a wonderful blessing that waters the grass, makes seeds grow, cleans the air, washes off house roofs, and gives trees a good shower bath. Did you ever go out and walk in a nice summer rain without an umbrella? Did you ever lift your face and feel the splatter of raindrops on your eyes and nose and cheeks? Sure, you're too mature to do that. But just try it sometime. Of course, you might think rain is a pain when you're on a picnic. But never disdain rain—because life without it would be a real drain!

Dear Lord, I must admit that I'm not as keen on dancing in the rain as I was when I could kick my heels higher but I do love that fresh smell everywhere after a nice soft rain. And I also love umbrellas. I have a small collection of them in my front hall, including one that has "Bernadette" painted on it, thanks to my love-to-shop sister who was always sending me unusual and wonderful gifts. Thank you, Lord for rain and umbrellas and sisters.

upper

Are you a member of the upper class, the upper crust, and accustomed to always getting the upper hand? If you are, then you may have "people" who take care of all your needs. But if you are like most of us, you probably know what it's like to often have an upside-down day, when anything that can go wrong, will. You know what it's like to take care of your own needs, re-right whatever went wrong, and turn the day from a downer to at least a better.

And in case you ever wondered where the phrase "upper crust" came from, it was in the middle ages when it became a polite custom to slice off the upper choice part of a fresh-baked loaf of bread and serve it to the king or to the ranking noble at the table. Aren't you glad that now you can get freshaked bread from a baker or make your own and slice your way into the upper crust whenever you want? Now you are old enough to have learned that one day you may be down in the dumps but the next day be up in the clouds. It all depends on the proper attitude adjustment.

Dear Lord, some people get down in the dumps and just stay there. They never try hard enough to find out how much fun it is to trick yourself into being "up in the clouds." Help them, Lord, to learn how to get the upper hand on down times.

"UPPER CRUST, MY DEAR"

vacuum cleaner

A vacuum cleaner is a "dust removing" machine that uses suction to suck up all the dirt from a carpet or a corner or a footstool. You probably have a vacuum cleaner in your house, but how would you like to have one that is as big as a refrigerator? That's how big the first vacuum cleaner was! The first commercial vacuum cleaner was invented by H. Cecil Booth in 1901. It was so big and heavy it took two men to operate it. Later a smaller vacuum cleaner was manufactured that looked like a bagpipe attached to a breadbox. It LOOKED funny but it not only helped clean up the country, it also improved health. The vacuum cleaner removed tons of germ-laden dust from offices, theater seats, shops, and homes. And during World War I, a vacuum even stopped a "spotted fever" epidemic! The fever was killing Navy men quartered in a large building and doctors thought germs might be in the dusty air. So that big refrigerator-sized vacuum was brought in to the rescue! And after it was used to vacuum the building, TWENTY-SIX TRUCKLOADS of dust were hauled away and buried. That ended the epidemic!

Now don't you feel better? No matter how much dust calls your house a home, it wouldn't take truckloads to haul it away. Many seniors have lived in one home for twenty, thirty, who-knows-how-many years. But even if you are a super cleaner-upper and your home could pass the white-glove test, there might be some dust balls hiding somewhere. And who cares? If you haven't had spotted fever recently, you could probably still win the Good Housekeeping Award of Approval. So give your vacuum a hug today and be grateful that it doesn't look like a bagpipe attached to a breadbox.

Dear God, I'm grateful that the Dust Police do not function in my precinct. I've been cleaning my house by sweeping each room with a glance but I really must get out that vacuum today. So thank you, Lord, for H. Cecil Booth, and for all who have invented things that make a desperate housewife's life a little easier.

variegated

As you know, variegated means multicolored, streaked, or dappled with different colors. A bouquet of all-yellow flowers is very pretty but a bouquet of variegated flowers—full of all different colors—is bright and interesting because of the variety. Have you ever seen an afternoon sky that was pretty but ordinary UNTIL sunset? THEN it became variegated with brilliant splashes of yellow, orange, pink, purple, and glittery gold. Could you imagine a sunset or a garden of flowers or a whole world that was all ONE color? Even if it was beautiful, it would finally get boring, wouldn't it? But God's world DOES change— seasons change from winter to summer, flowers go from bud to blossom, children grow up, grownups get more beautiful (?) with age. Never be afraid of changes. Trust in God's paintbrush and ask him to help you value the variegated.

Dear Lord, we can count on sunrise and sunset but in between there can be surprises—dark clouds, rain, sunshine, pain, lightning, laughter—and that's life! So help us welcome each day with open arms and open minds.

vinegar

"Old wives" always had a recipe or a cure for everything—and many of their concoctions included vinegar. They had vinegar cocktails and vinegar and honey tonics to heal a variety of things and then put vinegar to work around the house to clean, disinfect, and eliminate mold and mildew. They didn't know WHY vinegar worked but it often did. Now "scientific research" is beginning to praise the healing power of vinegar and other old-time tonics versus the wonder drugs that sometimes have powerful bad side effects.

From the Bible to Cleopatra to the Japanese Samurai warriors, vinegar was mentioned as a potent tonic to ensure strength and long life—so "being full of vinegar" was probably a compliment.

"DRINK THIS — YOU'LL FEEL BETTER"

The next time you hear someone say an old codger is still "full of vinegar," maybe he IS! Thanks to his "old wife's concoctions."

Dear Lord, I don't know who all those "old wives" were but they sure get credited with some strange cure-alls and some unusual but delicious recipes. So thank you, Lord, for wise old wives and new wives and in-between wives who all have their own special concoctions to keep a home and a family together.

voluntourism

Volunteering has long been a happy option for seniors who have the time and the desire to do something for others. Recently that idea has turned into something now being called "voluntourism." For those who like to travel, it's a combination vacation and a "give-back getaway." Several organizations are putting together packages that can take you to just about any country in the world or any state of the United States. No special skills are required but volunteers donate time, muscles, and know-how to work at a variety of jobs from monitoring elephant herds in Sri Lanka to tutoring children on an Indian reservation to helping build a Habit for Humanity home in one of many areas, either near or far away. Your accommodations might include camping in the countryside to staying at a high-end hotel. The participants might include a seventeen-year-old taking time off after high school, retirees older than seventy, or "young seniors" who retire early and have the time and the income to try "travel with a purpose."

Dear Lord, thanks for a program that is making a difference in a lot of lives. Of course, for many seniors, this program would not be physically or financially possible but it's a great idea and it might inspire some stay-at-homes to take a trip to a library, check out some books about a land of their dreams, and get temporarily "immersed" in a very different culture and lifestyle by becoming an armchair traveler.

ALL PACKED

walker

The term "walk" can mean to move about on foot or advance by steps. It can be used with other words or phrases: walk the dog; space walk; walk out (on strike); walk off with or walk away from. But when you turn it into "walker," it can indicate a person in a marathon OR a metal framework designed to help a person walk when they are having difficulty getting around on their own. These are words familiar to many senior citizens. When they are able, they walk for exercise or they just enjoy a walk in the park or in their own backyard. And when the legs begin to go, they can use a walker to KEEP on the go.

Walkers are like a lot of things useful to seniors—ice cream treats you can keep in your freezer so you don't have to run after the ice cream truck any more; glasses that help you see

near or far even if they are not rose-colored; friends that offe.
to give you a ride so you won't have to scrape the snow off your
windshield; frozen casseroles you can serve for dinner so you
don't have to spend all day shopping and chopping. Oh yes, in
senior years, there are a lot of ways to beat the system. You may
not like having to use a walker or settle for a frozen dinner instead of home-made but what the heck, when help is available,
grab it and run!

*Dear Lord, it's hard to make changes or to admit you
can't always do things exactly the same way you always
did before. But just doing things a little differently is a
small price to pay for keeping on keeping on! Thanks,
Lord, for all the helpers in today's modern world.*

warbler

A warbler is a bright-colored singing bird. These little songsters
are often called the "butterflies of the bird world" because they
are small, move fast, and have beautiful multicolored mark-
ings. In the summertime more than fifty kinds of warblers can
be seen flitting through the sunshine and fluttering in the tree
branches of North America, BUT in the winter, they vacation
in the tropics. Some of the warblers have interesting names.
There's the cerulean warbler, the red-faced warbler (who is
NOT embarrassed but DOES have a red face) and the prothonotary warbler. Did you know prothonotary can also mean the
chief clerk of a court or a chief secretary of a church? Do you
guess this bird has two careers—as a singer and a clerk, with

an office in a stump in a swamp somewhere? No, guess not, but it is a funny idea, isn't it? Do you like to sing or warble in the shower? If you do, why don't you think about joining the church choir? They are usually looking for some new voices. And then you could warble a joyful noise to the Lord!

Dear Lord, thanks for the beautiful warblers that deco-rate our world and for the singers who donate their time to join a church choir OR a chorus OR a barber-shop quartette—so we can have music to decorate our lives.

water

Water is that wonderful liquid that nobody can live without! It tastes so good when you're thirsty, and if you're VERY thirsty, nothing but water will do. But do you know how many atoms are in one drop of water? Well, if every person on earth joined together to count the atoms in one drop of water and each person counted one atom per second, it would take them thirty thousand years to finish counting. Can you imagine how tee-ny-tiny each atom must be? (And can you IMAGINE who took on the job and how long it took to figure out the answer to this one drop question? Don't ask!)

Anyway, do you ever have a day when you feel small and un-important? If you do, remember that every atom in that drop of water is important and without even ONE, the drop of water would be different. If something so infinitesimal is important to God's creation of water, think how important YOU must be to God—no matter what age you are!

Dear Lord, it amazes me how people have the time and the inclination to think about such things as "how many seniors would it take to screw in a light bulb?" or "how many bees would it take, working a twenty-four-hour shift, to manufacture a drop of honey?" or "how many drops of water would it take to make a really big splash when you spill it on the kitchen floor?" But what is even more amazing is just thinking of a list of the endless ways we use—and need—water every day. Thank you, Lord, for wonderful water.

whim

Did you ever have a whim, an idea, a fancy—to maybe do the donkey ride in the Grand Canyon or take lion-training lessons so you could join the circus or maybe even have raw fish, otherwise known as sushi, for dinner? They all sound pretty dangerous. But hey! This is only a whim. Maybe you'd rather whim-wham your way to a rain forest and listen to the music… the quick drumming of an orange-back woodpecker, the roar of a jaguar, the calls of tree frogs and hundreds of birds tweeting and twixting. No, wait, that sounds like a rock concert. You don't want to whim there. Or maybe you do. Well, we each have our own special whims from the time when we were about three years old and dressed up like a princess or a knight in shining armor or a lion tamer. Through the years, the whims change but it's good to stay whimsical. Then you can face life with a bang, not a whimper.

Dear Lord, aging is not always fun for those who are aging OR for those who live with them. That's why it's important to keep a little bit of whimsy in our lives. Someone once said that angels can fly because they "take themselves lightly"—and we should do the same.

wonky

Wonky is a British slang word that means shaky or tottery. When you've been sick in bed for a few days, the first day you get up and move around, you might feel a bit wonky. Sometimes when you watched the late movie or had a nightmare or just didn't get enough sleep for some reason, when the alarm goes off and you have to get up early, you might feel a bit wonky for a few minutes. And, let's be honest. If you are serious about being a senior citizen, you just might use wonky as an excuse whenever you don't want to do anything else. No, no, surely a senior would never do anything like that. BUT the older we grow, the more wonky might appear in our vocabulary. And that's OK. Shaky or tottery are words we might not like to use but Wonky is a British word and British words always sorta sound like fun.

Dear Lord, in senior years, some days we wake up full of vim and vigor, able to tackle chores in a single bound, powerful enough to go out for golf or lunch or even a guided tour somewhere. But then WHAM, out of no-where, along comes a wonky day. Oh well, thank you, Lord, for all the full-of-vigor days and all the wonky ones. Thank you for each new day you give us!

wordplay

Some witty people like to use wordplay in conversation and it's great fun to talk to them. Some seniors and others like to use wordplay to solve crossword puzzles. But the other day I received an e-mail with a word challenge. It said,

> Can you figure out what these seven words have
> in common?
>
> Banana   Dresser   Grammar   Potato
> Revive   Uneven   Assess

At first glance, maybe it was that they all had double letters in them. But no, it was a bit trickier than that. The answer was: In all the words listed, take the first letter of each word, place it at the end of the word, then read the word backwards and it will be the same word. Try it! Take the B from banana, put it at the end, read the word backwards, and you get banana again. Now isn't that silly to spend your valuable time solving e-mail word problems? No. Spending time on something that's fun is not a waste (especially when the answer to the problem is at the end of the e-mail message.)

If you work a crossword puzzle in the weekday newspaper, you only have to wait until the next day to see if you got all the answers right. Some of the large crosswords have the puzzle answers on another page or nearby so you don't even have to wait a day. Wouldn't it be great if all the problems in your life would come with the answers and if you tried to solve the puzzle by yourself without looking at the correct answers, at any time you could quickly check to see if you got it right? Well, I guess we have to admit that life is usually more work than play.

Dear Lord, I love working crossword puzzles. They are my favorite relaxer, second only to reading a good book. And yes, I know. I could be spending more of my time reading YOUR good book. But, Lord, your book doesn't always have the answers at the end.

work

Work is defined as an activity in which one exerts strength or faculties to do or perform something. So what does the word WORK have to do with seniors? You may be surprised to know that, for the first time since 1948, Americans aged sixty-five and up now outnumber teenagers in the workforce. Because they need the money or because they are bored with retirement, some of the fifty-plus folks are taking entry level, part-time jobs just like high school or college-age kids do. And employers say the seniors perform as well or even better in problem solving, adaptability, accuracy, and especially reliability. One "boss" said that people seem to think the oldest generation does not want any change but noted that they have lived through changes from World War II to the Worldwide Web and most have adapted well. In one workplace, four generations, from teens to seventy-plus, are working productively together. With supervisors who have been trained to manage multiple age groups, the eldest, the boomers, the GenXers, and the GenYers each bring something different to the mix and make a great team.

You may have had enough of "work" and are ready to enjoy time with family or friends or helping out at church or some charity, but it's interesting to see how each generation is capable of overlooking the stereotypes of others well enough to work together. Now if only the world could learn how "the work of many hands" joined as a team can banish stereotypes and lead to a joyful—and profitable—alliance.

Dear Lord, it's nice to see seniors who are physically fit taking small jobs like bagging groceries, part-time receptionist, office temp, paid baby-sitter, or whatever comes along. For those who enjoy working with others, it can make them feel like "they're in the game" again. And the extra cash can pay for fun extras. Thank you, Lord, for so many possibilities for today's ageless elders.

wriggle

Wriggle is a lot like wiggle and waggle. It means to twist and turn, jiggle and squirm. Did you ever do that? If you didn't, you must be the only person in the world who has learned how to NEVER ever get "antsy"! Sometimes whatever you are doing and wherever you are—in an office, in church or a theater, or just stretching out on your couch watching TV—you suddenly have the urge to move. You might not even realize it, but all of a sudden you're twitching muscles, moving your body, rolling your head, or tapping your foot—and maybe driving other people crazy! Why? Because wriggling is catching. As soon as someone sees you wriggle, they want to wiggle and waggle too. Do you feel like wriggling right now? Well, don't. See how long you can sit still without moving a muscle. It won't be easy but it's a good lesson in concentration. While you're sitting still, concentrate on how God made all your muscles and bones and nerves work together so you can stand and walk and reach and stretch—and wriggle.

Dear Lord, it gets harder to wriggle in and out of certain situations when you get older and sometimes we need to learn that lesson about concentration. Some experts on aging say that when you think you are forgetful, you are really just not concentrating as closely as you should. They say to FOCUS on each name or task and then you will remember it. I guess it's like prayer, Lord. I try to focus but soon I'm thinking what I'll cook for dinner or where I left my glasses. So help me, Lord, to concentrate on less wiggle and waggle and more on FOCUS.

X

X is a letter of the alphabet that sometimes stands alone without any other letters. People say "X marks the spot!" because a simple X is often used on a map to indicate a special place—like the spot where a buried treasure is hidden or the spot where you're going on vacation. And if you ever use Roman numerals (like telling which number this year's Super Bowl is) X equals ten. And if a person doesn't know how to write his or her name, even legal documents can be signed by simply writing an X instead of a signature. And people who DO know how to read and write sometimes end a love letter by adding an X to stand for a kiss. (Or they might put an X and an O which stands for a kiss and a hug.) But did you know that X is also used sometimes to stand for Christ (like in Xmas)? Do YOU always stand for Christ? When someone tries to get you to do something wrong, do you ever explain that it would not be Christian to do that? It's not always easy to "stand for" Christ and his teachings, but it IS always right—no matter how old you are. So the next time someone who doesn't know any better suggests you do something wrong, remember that X and what YOU stand for.

Dear Lord, I bet the editor didn't think I could come up with any X words but I did. Do you like this one, Lord?

X-ray

X-ray sounds like something from a science fiction story but of course, it's really something from a doctor's office or a hospital. Whenever someone is sick, a doctor examines the person's OUTsides but sometimes that's not enough and he has to use an X-ray machine to examine the person's INsides. Many seniors know more than they would like about hospitals—either as a visitor or a patient—but today's medical discoveries and treatments can heal much better than in past years. And X-rays are important because they help doctors find out where the problem is so they can figure out how to fix it.

Don't you sometimes wish you had an X-ray machine so you could look INSIDE the heads of some people you know to find out what in the world they are thinking? Well, there's something even better than an X-ray machine for that. It's called friendship. When you make a friend, you get to know

"Hmmm..."

each other so well, you often KNOW what each one is thinking. This is probably true with some of your oldest friends but
you know the saying "Old friends are gold, new ones are silver,"
so reach out and try to make some new friends too. You can
never have too many friends—even though you may never
know what SOME of them are thinking.

> *Dear Lord, families keep introducing seniors to new
> members—brides, babies, in-laws. But to widen a
> circle of friends may take a little shopping and open-
> mindedness. Younger friends can introduce elders to
> newer ideas, newer solutions to problems, newer out-
> looks and maybe even explain how to get on the inter-
> net. But seniors can share events and memories from
> the past that introduce the younger ones to some ideas
> and outlooks that may be oldies but goodies. It could
> turn out to be a win-win situation even without a per-
> sonal X-ray machine.*

xylophone

Xylophone is a musical instrument that is made of wooden bars
and played with wooden hammers. Maybe you've seen one or
even played one. Another musical instrument is similar to this
but it's made of METAL and it's called a GLOCKENSPIEL.
Both of these instruments have funny names but both are fun
to play or to hear played. Some PEOPLE have funny names
too, but you can't judge a person by a name or a house by
its front door. You might be surprised to find what's inside

a house or inside a person. Do you know anyone who has a very unusual name? Do you think the name fits him or her? If you were given a name that describes your personality, what would it be?

Dear Lord, some people might think Bernadette is an unusual name. It IS an old one (like me) but I have really enjoyed borrowing it from St. Bernadette. There were much stranger names in my family—Aunt Oskie, Uncle Pink, Aunt Linnie, Uncle Ezra, Uncle Ransom, and of course, Uncle Grover Cleveland. And my own sweet little Mama was saddled with the name Zella Hazel. She got rid of part of that name as fast as she could by passing it on to me, making me Zella Bernadette But don't tell anyone, Lord, that my first and legal name is Zella. I wouldn't like for that to get around.

yacht

Did you know yachts were once pirate ships? Yep, this recreational craft got its name from a type of speedy pirate ship of the sixteenth century that had the Dutch name Jacht (short for jachtschip or hunting ship.) A century later, British royalty found that this type of vessel made an excellent pleasure boat for cruising or racing and they called it Yaught, which finally became yacht.

The original Jacht engaged in robbery on the high seas. Today there's a different kind of piracy—stealing another's idea or invention or infringing on a copyright. Did you ever know someone who was that kind of pirate, someone who tried to "take credit" for your ideas or copied everything you did? If you got a new red car, they got a new red car, if you went on vacation to Hawaii, they went to Hawaii. They say imitation is a form of flattery but it can be very irritating. So if you get a yacht and your imitator then gets one, you can ease the irritation by telling yourself that THAT yacht is indeed a pirate ship.

Dear Lord, sometimes it's OK to follow someone's GOOD example, like if we try to follow the example of someone whose lifestyle or accomplishments seem admirable or maybe the example of some of the saints, but not someone just because they have a new red car or a yacht. (Actually, I don't know anyone who has a yacht or even a new red car so, Lord, you won't have to worry about me becoming a pirate!)

yawn

A yawn is something that happens when you don't expect it and can't stop it! Your mouth suddenly flies open and anybody who's looking thinks you must be tired or bored. Now that can be embarrassing in polite society. But did you know that many years ago, people were AFRAID of yawns? They thought if you opened your mouth wide, your life breath might escape and you'd fall over dead. So when they felt a yawn coming on, they immediately put a hand over the mouth so the breath would not escape. Today, people still put a hand over the mouth when they yawn—not because they're afraid but just to be polite.

Now that we know yawns are not dangerous, we also know they ARE contagious. As soon as you see someone else yawn, you want to yawn too, and if you're in a room full of people, pretty soon EVERYBODY wants to yawn. It's catching—just like measles, spotted fever, and a grumpy mood. When you're with someone who is all grumpy, you sometimes start to feel grumpy too. But when you're with someone who's all excited and enthusiastic, suggesting, "Let's go see that new movie!" or "Let's go on a picnic!" or "Let's make popcorn!" then you might start to feel excited about the idea too.

That's why even Christianity can be catching! Do you ever act so excited and enthusiastic about God's goodness and greatness and all God's wonderful creations and all the teachings and miracles of Jesus that other people get excited too—just from being with you? If you DO, you must have a lot of joy and gladness in your life. If you DON'T, maybe you should. Maybe you could start today.

Dear Lord, as we get older, sometimes it's hard to get as excited about things as we did when we were younger and full of beans, but it shouldn't. Sometimes we think we've seen it all and life is getting ho-hum. But wonders are all around. We just have to pay attention to see them and let that old enthusiasm kick back in.

yokel

The English green woodpecker was named the yokel because its call sounds like "yo-KEL, yo-KEL." Toward the beginning of the nineteenth century, people in England began calling country bumpkins yokels because they lived where the yokels sang. Today yokel is defined as a naïve or gullible inhabitant of a rural area or small town. But with television and the Internet, there are few "bumpkins" around and even if they are, it would not be nice to call anyone a yokel except maybe the English woodpecker.

Do you ever "label" someone because they come from a different culture or even a different neighborhood? Well, if you do, other people might start labeling you "rude, insulting, or maybe even a bigot." Of course, you would never do an awkward, unsophisticated thing like that, would you?

Dear Lord, it's so easy to mislabel others at first sight and some people even mislabel themselves, never giving themselves credit for their good qualities. Some may even label themselves "too old to do anything any more." Now isn't that a shame!

zap

No one is sure where this word came from but some say it was in an old comic strip, "Buck Rogers in the Twenty-fifth Century." Evidently Buck dealt with lots of strange enemies and would ZAP them with a ray gun. Today zap is a familiar slang word that often means to zap your dinner in the microwave. Wonder what Buck would have thought of that—zapping dinner instead of monsters.

Of course, sometimes those microwave dinners DO turn out to be monstrosities but they really help out when you need emergency food in a hurry. And folks of all ages often do need that—busy career people with little time to cook, kids home from school starving for a snack, and senior citizens who have stirred and measured and stewed and brewed so many meals they sometimes feel like they have "lost the will to cook." Yep, zap is a great word for today's hectic hurried world. And we're not even in the twenty-fifth century yet. How much faster and zappier can this world get!

Only Buck Rogers knows.

Dear Lord, thanks for all the modern meals today--fast-frozen, ready-made, deli-style, restaurant carry-out and of course, microwave. They sometimes do make life easier. And sometimes they are very good and even very nutritious, but somehow it seldom is as delicious as a good old home-made Mama's recipe.

zero

Zero is a nothing, a naught, of no value. They say it's good to be well-rounded, to know a little bit about a lot of things, but they also say that if you are totally rounded, you are a zero. Well, that's what I thought I would find when I got to the Z page in my old well-thumbed dictionary—zero words of interest. My dictionary has 1,378 pages—and gives only FOUR pages to the Zs—so what could I expect? As usual, I was surprised.

There's the word ZAFTIG which means a pleasingly plump lady. That's nice. ZANY means fantastically or absurdly ludicrous. I can relate to that. ZAZUELLA is described as a comic Spanish operetta. I'll have to take the book's word for that. ZEAL is eagerness and ardent interest. I can admire that.

ZEBRA is the black and white striped horse. Always good for a second look. Well, you'll just have to look up the rest yourself. But it just goes to showya how zero can lead to something more than naught.

If you ever have a zero day, with nothing to do, take a trip through a dictionary. See what it has to say about old-fangled, old hand, old school, old style, old-timer—and that should give you a few good laughs.

Dear Lord, the Zs may be near the back of the book but they go out with a zip-a-dee-do-dah zing! I love it.

zigzag

Zigzag is a series of short sharp turns in alternate directions—a criss-cross, a here and there, an up and down. By now, you have surely noted how I have zigzagged through this book—going from one regular word to an irregular one, from one silly thought to a serious one, from definitions to defamations, from explaining to editorializing, from facts to opinions.

But that's life—full of zigzags. One day you feel like singing, the next day you might feel like moping. One day life seems like a picnic, the next day it's the pits. Sometimes you feel like a nut, sometimes you don't. So look for the silver lining and all that jazz.

Sorry if I have zigged when I should have zagged at some places in this book but I hope I have given you more teehees than ZZZZZZZs.